HERBLOCK'S
HERE AND NOW

by Herbert Block

SIMON AND SCHUSTER, NEW YORK
1955

SECOND PRINTING

LIBRARY OF CONGRESS CATALOG CARD NUMBER: 55-12202

MANUFACTURED IN THE UNITED STATES OF AMERICA

PRINTED BY KONECKY ASSOCIATES, INC., NEW YORK

BOUND BY VAN REES PRESS, NEW YORK

2459

FOR *Bill and Rich*

CONTENTS

HERBLOCK'S
HERE AND NOW

1. MIRACLE INGREDIENT HP2x

WE'RE living in an era of slogans, symbols and smooth talk which may well go down in history as the Genuine Simulated Golden Age. Every time you turn on the radio or television somebody is telling how you, yes *you*, can get this wonderful, yes wonderful, gadget *now*, yes *now*, *yes* you can get it *now*—until you feel like hollering, "No, no, *no*—never!" And everything is so new, improved, increased and jam-packed with extra ingredients that it's enough to drive a guy to drink Plain Old Busthead, in the same old regular-size bottle.

When you hear a thing often enough I guess it penetrates, or at least sticks to the surface of the ears. I'm continually finding that I can sing—well, anyhow mumble—the complete lyrics of ding-dong ditties I don't really care for at all.

If it raps persistently, a phrase may be taken in by the mind, and vice versa; and the notion that goes unchallenged brings along its trunk and settles down to become a cliché. It's not hard to see how the people in George Orwell's *1984* came to live by crazy catch-phrases like "Ignorance Is Strength"—if you'd call that living. With enough advertising it might even be possible to popularize what somebody has suggested as the ultimate in slogans: "Cancer is *good* for you!"

Under the proper horrible circumstances you too could have your brain washed white as snow, leaving no tattletale gray matter. Even under ordinary circumstances you too can feel the soothing caress of nature's own baby-soft wool drawn tenderly across your delicate eyelids. All the irritating connotations are filtered out by special copywriting processes, and everything is improved by Miracle Ingredient HP2x (Hocus-pocus twice multiplied).

Ordinary old-fashioned hocus-pocus has always been with us. The amazing quick-action job of Miracle Ingredient HP2x is that it performs a slick-as-a-whistle conversion of ordinary hogwash into rich sudsy stuff which produces an authentic-looking luster, sparkling with simulated sincerity.

I don't like it, and my particular beef—without any special tenderizing—is smooth, velvety Political HP2x.

I object when the product runs a poor second to the packaging, and when the appearance of quality or sincerity takes the place of quality and sincerity. Of course, this isn't entirely new either. The old patent-medicine peddlers used to roll their eyes and beat their chests. But the pitch was less subtle and insidious.

The miracle-ingredient men have learned about people what Pavlov discovered about dogs—that symbols alone can produce reactions, even after they've been separated from the things they're supposed to represent. Cartoonists use symbolic devices more than most people, and perhaps some of us should take the Penitent Sackcloth-and-Ashes out of Bin No. 45 and cover ourselves with them for banging the symbols too hard. Politicians have learned to filter out the obvious irritants and make HP2x even easier to absorb.

For example, if cigar smoking suggests "politician," the irritating cigar can be replaced by a pipe, which—as symbols go—makes the face that holds it appear more thoughtful; or if he wants to use drastic measures, the politician can give up smoking altogether. But this doesn't remove the politics. If "striped-pants diplomacy" becomes an opprobrious term, the cutaway outfit can be replaced by a sack suit and sweater. But if there is stuffing inside the shirt, the packaging hasn't changed anything.

Silk hats provide as easy a target for charges of "big-business government" as they do for snowball-throwing boys in cartoons. But business is business, in top hat, Homburg or lightweight felt. A fellow can be for hard money in a soft shirt or for high tariffs in a low collar. Things are not always what symbols have made them seem.

Politicians have also learned something else from the miracle-ingredient men—that a defect, if made conspicuous enough and promoted as a virtue, can actually be capitalized on. If the color imprinting machine goes haywire on a batch of golf balls, there's no use tossing them aside when you can advertise that these are the *only* golf balls with easy-to-see identifying marks *all over* them. That would be fair enough if people liked the idea, but in politics the same technique can be pretty tricky.

If a politician made a sly deal to give away a public park to a muckle manufacturer, they would both be exposed, the public would get mad, and they would get what they deserved for being so dumb. The irritating ingredient is the exposure. This can be easily eliminated by performing the transaction publicly and pointing to it with pride.

The thing for the mayor to do is to hire a band, hand over a ribboned key and make a speech boasting of the splendid action taken in removing this park from the hands of tax-eating bureaucrats. He can say he has hurled back a threat of socialism and can go on to praise the unselfish civic devotion of the manufacturer who is assuming the burden of paying taxes on this property, chopping down the trees, and erecting a muckle factory which will increase the prosperity of the community. Of course the kids won't have the park to play in any more, but later on they can work in the muckle factory and build their own private parks with enterprise and good old know-how.

That takes the whole thing out of the low-skulduggery class and puts it on a high-policy plane. It's even better if the mayor and the muckle manufacturer believe their own speeches, which is not too difficult. HP2x, wonder worker that it is, gets right into the blood.

When a fellow wants to beat his conscience to death he can always take the righteous attitude that conscience jabbed him first, and there are few things that can't be rationalized by people who are really willing to roll up their minds and work at it.

There's a certain amount of HP2x in a lot of what passes for objectivity. Used here, it removes unattractive choices by forming a soft emulsion which feels as smooth and creamy on the one hand as it does on the other hand. Specifically, I mean the pious, chin-stroking type of opinion ' which surveys both sides of any conflict, purses its lips, places its finger tips together and invariably decides that there is much to be said on both sides.

If you say, "My, the grass looks nice and green," and somebody shouts, "You're crazy—the color of grass is purple," some synthetic Solomon will always come forward to look wise, assume an air of great judiciousness, and announce that these are obviously extreme positions, between which lies the truth. There will also come forward, possibly from between the cracks in the sidewalk or wherever they have been hiding during the Great Grass Debate, a host of others who will hail this as true wisdom—an eminently fair decision because it favors neither one side nor the other. And the only argument then will be about where to place the statue of the New Solomon.

If there were a series of cases involving adults kicking babies around, the same type of phony judiciousness would—if it came to any conclusions at all—support the babies in half the cases and the adults in the other half. This would also show a complete absence of discrimination or bias, and would be almost as dispassionate as it was dishonest.

I don't know what's so fascinating about the "middle of the road," but for a lot of people this position has the kind of magnetic attraction that a coffee cup has for cigarette ashes; and it's regarded as the ideal place to dump any kind of decision. I

6

guess it sounds as if it were solid. But it's often the worst possible place to be. And in a choice between right and wrong, I think something better than a middle-of-the-road policy is needed.

The miracle ingredient sometimes gets into political commentary, where it looks more nonpartisan than nonpartisanship itself. The middle-of-the-road technique here is to lay about on both sides with exactly even vigor or gentleness at all times, regardless of issues and regardless of who is to blame for what. Under this formula you could mark the calendar in advance, making a policy of criticizing Democrats on Mondays, Wednesdays and Fridays, and Republicans on Tuesdays, Thursdays and Saturdays. This would insure administering chastisement with an even, if somewhat clammy, hand; and it would leave Sundays to pray for the Republic.

That's also a lot of HP2x. It would certainly *look* independent all right; but it would actually be the abandonment of independence and honest judgment. It would be sacrificing principle for appearances and adopting the very expediency that needs criticism in politics. It could also be, and sometimes is, the sleaziest kind of partisanship, helping to diffuse the blame when a particular group of politicians needs to be reminded of its duty.

During the middle of the Eisenhower Administration a friend on another paper suggested one day that I do a cartoon kicking hell out of Adlai Stevenson. I mentioned that since Stevenson wasn't in office there didn't seem to be any occasion for criticizing him, unless he had said something that seemed to call for it. I asked what the criticism should be. The friend, who only wanted to be helpful, couldn't think of anything. He just felt that since I was sometimes critical of President Eisenhower, this would show a nice balance. I suppose it would, in about the same way as putting a hand on the butcher-shop scales.

Other readers have told me that during the early years of the Truman Administration the cartoons were tougher than those during a similar period under Eisenhower. I don't know whether that's so or not, but I think that the Democrats, after long years in office, learned to roll with the punches a little better.

I've operated on the simple theory that criticism should be

dealt out when and where it seemed most needed, without trying to keep score or make everything come out even. When
McCarthy (R) and McCarran (D) were both active in the same
line of work, cartoons were devoted to both of them. But things
don't always work out in that bipartisan way, and I can't stack
the characters, the issues, or the smears to make things balance
politically. It would be phenomenal if each party was right—
or if an observer thought each was right—an equal number of
times during any period, particularly when one party at a time
had most of the responsibility for governing.

The cartoons that I've done about the last couple of administrations have probably been toughest when the popularity of each
was highest. And when an administration seems to be motivated
by expediency and a willingness to sacrifice principles to "avoid
trouble," I think it's the job of editorial people to show them
they can get into even more trouble by doing the wrong thing
than by doing what's right. That should make it easier for them
to do the right thing, but I doubt that they ever appreciate our
efforts along this line.

Politicians can't please everybody in their work any more than
I can in mine; and it's a mistake to try. "Unity" is a nice appeal-
ing word, but unless there's unity on principles, it doesn't mean
anything. As the old gag goes, the lion and the lamb can always
lie down together—with the lamb inside. It's no good that way.

I can always draw a picture of Uncle Sam and John Public
looking up at the Stars and Stripes and saying, "Let's all be
Americans!" A cartoon like that might offend nobody; even the
most rabid extremists could feel that they represented the Ameri-
canism I was plugging—and a lot of people would think it was
terrific. But it wouldn't mean anything either.

It's the same way with speeches. If you say you're for the Con-
stitution of the United States, everyone will be right with you.
If you narrow it down a little and say you're for the Bill of Rights,
a pair of dark eyebrows might twitch. If you get still more specific
and say that the rights guaranteed under the First and Fifth
Amendments must continue to protect everybody, a pair of eyebrows might go up. If you go on to say that the Attorney General

should be more vigorous in upholding these rights, a couple of pairs of eyebrows will turn to each other, silently asking whether this talk is proper for mixed company—which is to say, Republicans and Democrats. And if you say that the President has a responsibility to see that this is done, somebody is going to wonder whether what this fellow has to say is really in good taste at all. But it's only when you stop generalizing and start being specific that you're getting the marbles out of your mouth.

I think independence not only has to avoid a slavish effort to follow a political party line; it also has to avoid a slavish effort to stand in the middle or off to one side. It has to decide what it thinks is right in each case, regardless of whether it seems to agree with one side or another. In doing this it has to run the risk of being accused, by partisans, of partisanship.

In introducing the reader to what follows in this volume, I won't say, "I'm not one to criticize, *but—*"

I *am* one to criticize and have been doing it for years. It's not unpleasant work either, even though it doesn't get a fellow outdoors as much as he'd like.

I can remember a time not so many years ago when criticism of government and jokes about public officials and policies were supposed to be good for us. In those days the cry was for more and more criticism. I find it hard to believe that this stuff, which until recently was yummy, delicious, packed with character-building vitamins, and sometimes even enriched with political arsenic, has now become bad bad bad, even in nontoxic form and comparatively mild doses. And I can not get it through my head that insecurity is security, or that politics is not politics.

It never seemed to me that any President or major party was hell-bent on turning our country over to our enemies, or that any of our officials came straight from Olympus either. I didn't enter into the competition for the National Open Rock-Throwing Championship and haven't been an active participant in the Tournament of Roses either. In this respect perhaps I'm a middle-of-the-roader, or maybe I'm in a rut. But with the passing years I don't seem to be able to make the sharp turns very well.

It was the girl in *My Sister Eileen* who said, after trying to live on cereal samples, "I'm tired of roughage. What I want is a little *smoothage*." Some observers have felt that after a long diet of political roughage the country is in the mood for a "breathing spell." But the same fellows who talked up that roughage stuff can't tell me now that we should live on nothing but smoothage. Honest criticism can't have become unhealthy all of a sudden.

Perhaps we're in an "Era of Good Feeling." But after the Depression, World War II, and the years of smears, what we have been in lately may be not so much an Era of Good Feeling as an Era of Feeling Numb, in which anybody who does not happen to be named Joseph R. McCarthy is likely to be regarded as a great statesman.

I certainly wouldn't condemn an entire major party, as some have tried to do; nor would I endorse all the members of one, as President Eisenhower did.

There are fine men in both parties, and some of them have served under administrations of both. As a matter of fact, looking back over appointees like Henry L. Stimson, John Sherman Cooper, Frank Knox, John Winant, John J. McCloy, Warren Austin, Robert Patterson and others, it sometimes seems to me that we had better Republicans in government under the Democrats than we've been getting under the Republicans.

Administrations change; "alphabet agencies" move out and advertising agencies move in. But in my stuff the formula is still the same. It tries to filter out nothing but HP2x itself—through a non-secret process which involves a few grains of ordinary salt—and it occasionally includes some old-fashioned irritants.

All of us who engage in commentary—which takes in the entire population if you include those with amateur standing along with the ones who get paid for the pleasure of popping off—hope that we may someday produce a small pearl of wisdom. And where would the pearl industry be without irritating ingredients?

"That's The Kind We Want—You Can See Just What He's Not Thinking"

12/29/1954

2. THE INSECURITY SYSTEM

WHEN Pierre L'Enfant laid out the city of Washington, D. C., in 1791 he was not trying to create a center of confusion. That came later with the invention of things like the automobile, carbon

11

paper, and what I keep calling the Internal Insecurity Program.

It was M. L'Enfant's idea, as any Washingtonian will explain to the hapless tourist who finds himself on a motoring merry-go-round, that the many circular intersections would provide strategic points to mount cannon in case of revolution. Whether or not M. L'Enfant should have been stood in front of his own cannon, as motorists have often muttered, is irrelevant and besides it's too late now, anyhow.

The point is that in planning the seat of government he was apparently worried about an entirely different danger from that which concerned the men who planned the government itself. They were thinking about the need to protect the people from the government, rather than the government from the people. In fact, it was their idea that "Governments are instituted among Men" to secure "certain unalienable Rights."

I don't want to make a historical fall guy of M. L'Enfant, who was not designing a government and who did lay out a beautiful city. But, figuratively speaking, what's happened in recent years is that the L'Enfant idea has been nudging out the Jefferson idea in government itself. And this has had *everybody* going around in circles.

For several years now, the government has been biting its nails over possible subversive ideas, and glancing nervously up and down the avenues and inside people's heads. No cannon have been mounted, but there's been plenty of firing—and at the merest drop of a remark. Whatever the state of our defenses against possible foreign aggressors, the American government has probably never been so firmly on guard against Americans.

Loyal American citizens have been denied passports to visit other free countries for fear they might keep a rendezvous with an alien idea, or that instead of just taking in the views they might also give out with some. And distinguished travelers from abroad have been denied entrance to our country for fear they might say something which would unseat what officials seem to regard as the feeble and tottering reason of the American people.

The Attorney General of the United States, in his boundless zeal to protect the government from anything which protects

The Recording Angels

3/14/1955

the rights of individuals, has modestly requested that he be empowered to authorize taps on telephones at his own discretion.

Approximately ten million people in government, the armed

"Sh—We're Busy"

4/7/1955

The Knock At The Door

5/17/1955

14

forces and defense industries are directly affected by the Internal Security Program, under which they can be bounced out of their jobs, branded as suspicious characters and rendered unemployable for other jobs on the basis of the slightest bit of gossip—and without knowing who or what hit them.

Under this system—and I use the word laughingly—thousands of patriotic men and women have had the boom lowered on them for "wrong ideas," "wrong associations," "bad morals," "bad judgment" and "bad habits"—or, rather, whatever various officials choose to mean by such terms. As far as I know, nobody has been classified as a security risk because of bad breath, but this hazard may well be included in one of many vague categories.

The Defense Department, apparently realizing that there has been some injustice in all this, proposed to improve the security situation by making the program apply also to people in "defense-related" industries. This would provide a kind of equality by insuring that just about everybody in the country would come under the same ax. What could be fairer?

As the late Milt Gross might have asked, "Is this a system?" I happen to have a ready answer. It's not a system and it's not security. Aside from the fact that it gives individuals about the same kind of security as that of tin ducks in a shooting gallery, and that the injustices that have occurred under this program would by now fill a library, it doesn't give us anything to feel comfortable about as a nation either.

The effect of the program on individuals leaving the government was well illustrated in a cartoon by Alan Dunn in *The New Yorker* in which an applicant for a job with a business firm explains to the potential employer, "It's true, sir, that the State Department let me go, but that was solely because of incompetence."

Unfortunately for the national security, this would not be a typical case because the program practically puts a premium on incompetence. The egghead is a prime object of suspicion, but the fathead is a good bet to stay on for a gold watch and pension. If a fellow has never done any thinking at all, there's no problem about what he might have thought at some time in the past. And from the standpoint of the department head or security officer concerned with playing it safe for himself, that's the type that involves the least "risk."

At a time when the government needs the best brains it can get, this wouldn't seem to be the safest way to play it for the country; but a guy has to think about keeping his own job, doesn't he? Under this program, security has become the business of everybody—for himself.

The trouble began with a built-in boner in the loyalty-security program adopted under the Truman Administration in 1947—the fact that the system permitted reliance on information by anonymous accusers, or, as Justice Douglas has termed them, "faceless informers."

It would be difficult to devise a system which would create more confusion or provide a greater field day for cranks, unscrupulous underlings, vindictive neighbors, malicious acquaintances—and, for that matter, Communists, if they wanted to get rid of worth-while people in government. It would, as I say, have been difficult to devise a worse system—but not impossible, especially for a new administration, full of energy and bent on surpassing the old. The Eisenhower Administration managed it.

In the early part of 1953, when it was announced that the old loyalty-security system was on the way out, there was a flicker of hope that things would get better. This proved to be one of the shortest-lived flickers on record, and it was not long before the simple stupidities of the earlier system began to seem like the good old days.

The new program, which retained the anonymous informants but eliminated the old appeal boards and tossed everything into one big "security-risk" stewpot, was presented as being "improved" and "more effective," like a patent medicine or a cake mix. This new, improved formula, flavored with cynicism and enriched with generous juicy gobs of politics, dispelled the nasty, nagging, queasy feeling induced by the old program and replaced it with genuine sure-nuff national nausea.

Washington became more than ever a Wonderland, with everybody wondering who and what next? Security methods became,

"Here We Go Again"

4/29/1953

to use Alice's words, "curiouser and curiouser." But we did not become securer and securer.

As a matter of national security, you might think an able for-

"Now We've Got A Man Who'll Turn His Back On Anybody"

11/11/1954

eign service would be indispensable to the country. But it hasn't been indispensable to a State Department eager to "avoid trouble" by tossing overboard some of its most faithful and competent men. One of these was John Paton Davies, an outstanding career man of twenty-three years' experience.

Mr. Davies' case was important enough to come to the personal attention of Secretary Dulles, who decided that while Mr. Davies had not in any way been disloyal, he was nevertheless guilty of "bad judgment." Apparently he'd had the bad judgment to give an honest appraisal of the Chiang Kai-shek regime some years before—and the even worse judgment to keep on serving the government during a period when there was a demand by some senators that good heads like his should be served up on platters.

In a word-association test, "national security" might evoke from many people the response "atom bombs." At any rate, it would certainly seem that our continued scientific progress had something to do with our capacity for defense. But you'd hardly know it from the workings of a security program which continues to accentuate the negative and eliminate the positive—including such positive contributors to national defense as atomic scientists who were responsible for our getting the bomb in the first place. Among these was Dr. J. Robert Oppenheimer. In the process of dropping him from government as a security risk, a special board decided that he had not been disloyal or unco-operative but that he had failed to display sufficient "enthusiasm" for the hydrogen-bomb proposal.

This set still another new criterion for security and suggested the possibility of scientists and other government workers taking an oath to be "trustworthy, loyal, helpful, friendly, courteous, kind, obedient, cheerful, thrifty, brave, clean, reverent—and enthusiastic."

I wonder whether, if the present internal-security methods had been in operation in 1944, we would have developed the atomic bomb at all. Some of the biggest contributions to that project were made by "foreigners" like Einstein and Fermi, who might not even have been admitted to this country under the McCarran Internal Security Act. Certainly Dr. Einstein's views and associations would have made him a "security risk" under the present program, along with Oppenheimer and others.

"I Hear There's Something Wrong With Your Morale"
2/16/1954

I'd guess that such a project, involving such people, would not have raised any cheers in the government of today—particularly since it involved the spending of more than two billion dollars without any assurance that it would succeed.

But it did succeed, partly because of the imagination and daring of Franklin D. Roosevelt—and because it was still thought in those days that the security of this nation depended on the brains and energy and courage of the people that it could draw upon, and not upon the number of people who could be barred from service to it.

Incidentally, the scientists don't seem to be the fuzzy-minded fellows they are so often pictured as being by people with fuzzy ideas. There is probably no group that has seen more clearly or spoken up more forcefully about dangers to the country. Poli-

"Odd How Many Of Them Drop Out, Isn't It?"

12/15/1954

"Who's Being Walled Off From What?"

4/15/1954

6/3/1954

ticians might well envy the clarity of Dr. Vannevar Bush, who said, for example, in a speech in December 1953:

> Ruthless, ambitious men are using government loyalty procedures for political purposes. The most important objective of our enemy is to spread confusion and distrust among us . . . but we are carrying on the process now without prompting.

Of course, the security program hasn't been limited to science and statecraft. It involves every part of the executive branch including the Department of Agriculture, which is not noted for its secret weapons.

This department also has done some dirt-farming in the security field, and got into the act publicly when it plowed under our foremost expert on Asian agriculture and land reform, Wolf Ladejinsky. With this effort it managed to surpass even the State Department, which had employed him before he was transferred to Agriculture.

Mr. Ladejinsky had served abroad so effectively for the United States—and against Communism—that he had won the high praise of Asians and non-Asians alike—of Ambassadors and former Ambassadors, Republican and Democratic, of General Douglas MacArthur, among many others, and of the Japanese Government, which appealed to Secretary Benson to keep him on the job in Asia.

Despite these testimonials and despite Ladejinsky's full clearance by the State Department, Secretary of Agriculture Benson dropped him as a "security risk."

For the benefit of those who have wondered about the strange and mysterious things that must go on in the minds of some of the government security officers, a peep into one of the dimmer caverns was provided with the publication of a statement by John Glen Cassity, security chief of the Department of Agriculture.

Mr. Cassity called attention to the fact that Ladejinsky had been born in Russia—which was well known—and that he still had sisters in Russia—which was also well known, as was the fact

"That's No Eagle"

10/20/1954

**"Now Don't Be Afraid
To Speak Frankly"**

11/9/1954

"Looks Like A New Kind Of Plowing-Under Program"

12/23/1954

that Ladejinsky had not been in touch with them for about nine years. He then said of Ladejinsky's anti-Communist work (hang on here because it may make your head spin) that his articles "were anti-Communist enough for Tass [the Russian news agency] to attack them." And "those anti-Communist articles alone would have been enough to bother me when you consider that this man had relatives in Russia."

The Department of Agriculture claimed—and Ladejinsky promptly denied—that he had once been a member of two subversive organizations.

But the case didn't end there. After Agriculture had dropped Ladejinsky, Harold Stassen, then head of the Foreign Operations Administration, employed him and sent him to Indochina, where he continued serving the U. S. in a delicate mission. Mr. Stassen received as little support from the White House this time as he did before when he had attempted to stand up to McCarthy. I can hardly classify myself as one of Mr. Stassen's ardent admirers, and do not regard him as a consistent champion of civil liberties and justice; but in these cases, at least, he looked like a knight in armor in a parade of pussycats.

When bewildered newspaper correspondents asked President Eisenhower about this security conflict he gave it as his opinion that *everybody* was right in the Ladejinsky case—that a man could be regarded as a security risk by one department but found okay for work in other and more sensitive departments.

This recalls the story of the two friends, crossing the country in opposite directions, who chanced to meet when each was changing trains at Chicago. They became engrossed in conversation, and while talking they both boarded the same train together. After they had reminisced a while longer, one of them looked out the window of the speeding train, smiled and said, "Ah, it's a great age we're living in. Here you are going to California, and I'm going to New York—and we're both on the same train!"

It's a great security system we're operating under. Until he finally reversed himself after seven months, here was Mr. Benson going one way; here were Mr. Dulles and Mr. Stassen going the other way; and here was Mr. Eisenhower apparently trying to go both ways at once. And all of them on the same train—wherever *that* might be going.

Final returns on this case came nine months after the suspension, when Secretary Benson, appearing before a Senate subcommittee investigating security procedures, admitted that security considerations were not the real reason for dropping Ladejinsky. He conceded that the security charges were "gratuitous and unnecessary." And in what may have been the understatement of the year, he said, "As we look back on it now it probably would have been best if it (referring to the security angle) had not been injected into it."

But men like Ladejinsky and John Paton Davies have been, as

"Yaaaa—We've Got More Security Than You Have"

1/3/1955

these cases go, pretty lucky. They were sufficiently prominent to make news, and the stories about them aroused public indignation. We never hear about most security cases. Few victims feel they can afford either the ugly publicity or the costs in time and money involved in fighting their cases.

One who paid the price for clearance was Mrs. Beatrice Murphy Campbell, an employee in the Veterans Administration, who, in April 1955, wrote a newspaper article describing a four-month nightmare which began when she was called to her Division Chief's office one afternoon. There she met a Director of Personnel who asked her to sign her acknowledgment of a paper. Then, in her words:

> He handed me the letter, looked at his watch and announced, "As of this minute you are suspended from your job. I will escort you back to your desk to pick up your personal belongings. You will turn over your building and other passes, and I will see you out the door of the building."

The charge against her turned out to be that she had "reportedly" been at one time a member of the Washington Bookshop Association, which was later put on the Attorney General's List.

As a suspended employee trying to clear herself, Mrs. Campbell was obliged to support herself with no current income, and to pay the cost of a lawyer besides. She was temporarily unemployed but not unoccupied, as the defense was a full-time four-month chore. She went on to say:

> In the first week of my suspension, my lawyer wrote to the agency asking for particulars. What was the (supposed) definite date of my membership? Who made the charge? And so on. Three days before the expiration of the thirty allowed me for replying to the letter of suspension, he received a letter saying that no information could be given.
>
> Had my lawyer and I been able to pinpoint the date in those two years (1940-41) we could have saved much

11/25/1953

work, worry and expense. But when he pressed for a definite date he was told to "just cover from 1940 on." Try reconstructing 14 years of your life!

"Welcome, Friend—Put 'Er There"

8/29/1955

Mrs. Campbell was, in an **ironic way,** also more fortunate than many alleged security risks. It was her great "luck" that for many years past she had been the victim of spinal arthritis, for which

2459

"Dear, I Still Think We Should Have Had This Cleared With The Department"

12/17/1954

she is still forced to wear a cast. And she was able to prove she could not have committed the frightful offense of joining the book club fourteen years before— partly because at that time she had been ill in bed, fighting for her life.

The "evidence" in this case turned out to be based on something that happened five years before, when an FBI man interviewed Mrs. Campbell about a friend of hers seeking government employment. The friend had been an early member of the bookshop who had later resigned—and had stated all this in her application. The FBI man concluded the interview with Mrs. Campbell by writing down an account of their conversation, which she signed without reading. Mrs. Campbell continues:

> Not until the paper was presented as evidence did I know that what it said was the FBI man's interpretation of our interview. It read: "I joined the Bookshop with ——— in 1940 to take advantage of the discounts."
>
> Without my opening my mouth, every word of the statement was proven false.

Sometimes it seems like lily-painting to attempt cartoons caricaturing such a system.

I tried to do a pictorial *reductio ad absurdum* in the cartoon of the Foreign Service officer and the Christmas cards, and hoped it was, in a wry way, amusing. The next day I heard from a former government employee who was curious as to where I got the idea for this drawing. It turned out that he had been employed abroad by the State Department for several years—and had, of course, been fully cleared. But later, when he tried to get a job with the Army Signal Corps, he was asked if he kept in touch with any people abroad. He replied that he didn't correspond at all—just sent out a few Christmas cards each year. Whereupon they said, "Let's see your Christmas-card list."

P.S.: He did not get the job.

"Hurry Up With That Dragon. The Audience Is Getting Impatient"

2/22/1954

3. TELL ME NOT IN MOURNFUL NUMBERS

ONE OF THE greatest aids in the art of hocus-pocus is the use of meaningless numbers. For impressiveness, numbers are probably second only to serious-looking male models dressed up in medical jackets. The latter have not yet been used in politics but are probably being held in reserve to give eminent television testimony against a good health-insurance bill, if one should come up.

It's not necessary for the numbers to be particularly relevant to anything. It's only necessary that they should be pronounced distinctly, slowly and solemnly.

In May 1955 a Hoover Commission report on inefficiency in the armed forces declared that the Navy had on hand 886,000 pounds of canned hamburger, and said that at the current rate of consumption this was enough to last for sixty years.

Eight hundred and eighty-six thousand pounds! Sixty years! Those were certainly numbers to think about, but not too much. The consumption of canned meat in the Navy in peacetime naturally is low. But the 886,000 pounds could be disposed of in exactly one day by feeding each of the Navy's 886,000 men an eight-ounce service portion of canned hamburger at each of two meals. I'm not arguing that the Navy was stockpiling efficiently or inefficiently. I'm only saying that the numbers put out by the Hoover Commission contained more uncanned bologna than 165,000,000 people could swallow at current rates of consumption.

The words "bigger" and "better" are often linked together, and in a fast shuffle they can be made to sound like one and the same thing. This is what might be called the quantitative theory of quality. If it's bigger it must be better. Thus the Senate Committee on Government Operations reported an increase in the number of hearings held in 1953 over those held under the previous leadership in 1952. Its chairman further presented figures to show that his committee had questioned 320 people in 123 closed hearings in that year, as against only nine witnesses interrogated in six closed hearings the year before. The fact that these grillings were a national disgrace was a minor matter. There was an *increase* in them.

Elaborate maps and charts have been drawn to show the distances traveled by public officials, as if statesmanship was something measured on a mileage meter. Let no one be dastardly enough to ask, "Were these trips necessary?" The point is that the miles traveled, laid end to end, would reach part way to the moon. If some of those peripatetic officials actually *went* to the moon, that would be something, particularly if they stayed there. But miles traveled, just as miles, don't thrill me very much, particularly when I don't get to take in any of the scenery.

We needn't go into detail here on numbers-which-don't-go-into-detail. It is enough to cite only the High Flying Percentage Figure and the Footless Statistic. An example of the former is the proud claim that a Congress has passed, say, 80 per cent of a President's program—which may have been 95 per cent inadequate to start with or which may have been passed with 99½ per cent modifications—or 50 per cent of which possibly shouldn't have been passed at all.

Columnist Bill Gold, who was probably the first to publish the final score on the Navy hamburgers, also discovered a beautiful example of the Footless Statistic, a hardy but elusive type which subsists entirely on holes from domestic Swiss cheese and has not a leg to stand on.

Early in 1953 it was said by various officials that since Inauguration Day government employees were getting to work twenty-seven minutes earlier in the morning, as proved by checking the flow of cars coming into Washington. Mr. Gold, who is not only fond of figures but even fonder of facts, took the trouble to do a little checking himself, and called the highway departments of the District of Columbia, Maryland and Virginia. His check showed that, as far as anyone knew, there had been no variation in the traffic at all. He also phoned the government officials who

"We Caught A Whale
But It Shrank"

3/3/1954

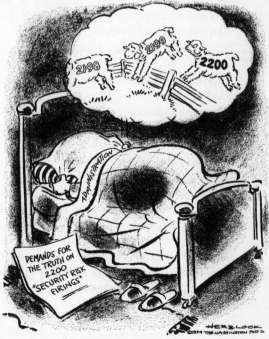

"Oh, No—Not That
Number Again"

2/8/1954

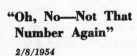

had used this bit of mythology in speeches, and each of them had—alas—heard it only from some other politician. But his published account of this statistical folderol did not keep others from continuing to use the Footless Statistic, and it still pops up in speeches as an example of efficiency, if not of factuality.

There is an art in the use of numbers, as illustrated by the old story of the man who went to the jokesmiths' convention. These gagsters knew all the jokes so well that they had them catalogued and numbered, and when a member told a funny story he simply said "908," or "56" or whatever its number was, whereupon the rest of the jokesters responded with laughter and applause. The guest, unexpectedly called upon to speak, was at a loss until the member who was his host whispered to him to say "904," which represented a particularly appropriate story. But when he spoke it he was greeted by cold silence. "I thought," he complained to his host, "you said that was a good story." "It *is*" was the reply. "But it's the way you *tell* it."

With political numbers also, much depends on the way they are told. Numbers have been much used in connection with national security; and, properly told, they are even supposed to take the place of evidence and trial by jury. If there were safety in numbers we'd be sitting pretty, because we've had plenty of them.

In 1950, on different days, a certain senator held in his hand a list of 205 or 81 or 57 people who were employed by the State Department or not employed by it, and who were Communists— or were *not* Communists, or something. One of the most effective uses of numbers since then occurred in the famous joint television appearance of Attorney General Brownell and J. Edgar Hoover in November 1953.

Shortly before, Mr. Brownell, in a prepared public speech, had said that President Truman had knowingly appointed to office a Communist spy. The man alleged by Brownell to be a Communist spy was Harry Dexter White, who had been dead for some five years at that time. The charge of treason, or something awfully close to it, against a former President of the United States did not go very well, and Mr. Brownell then decided that he

11/13/1953

didn't quite mean his charge to sound the way he had meant it
to sound. But he and Mr. Hoover appeared before a Senate subcommittee—headed by Senator Jenner, who had himself accused

George C. Marshall of being a traitor — to explain with more detail and drama.

They said in this hearing that during the Truman Administration Mr. Hoover had sent to the White House a 71-page memorandum on espionage in which Mr. White had been mentioned in three places, and later a 28-page memorandum containing information about Mr. White from 30 different sources. Those were certainly good numbers, although neither the 30 different sources nor the texts of the 28-page and 71-page reports were revealed.

I don't know whether White was guilty of anything or not. And since no conclusive evidence was disclosed I may never know. But I felt at the time—as I still do—that guilt by association is not good enough, that guilt by numerology is not good enough, and that an Attorney General who uses those methods is not good enough either.

At the conclusion of his television performance, Brownell said that he had made his accusations because he believed in freedom of information. And following that noble statement, this believer in freedom of information declined to hold any press conferences for the next nine weeks.

When he finally unbolted his door to the press, it turned out that his memory was by this time a little hazy about some aspects of the White case, and the questioning revolved around another number he had referred to in his testimony: 1,456.

This was the figure which the Administration had given out, for an opening shot in the famous Political Numbers Game, as the number of people who had been separated from the government under its security-risk program. The security mills were grinding pretty fast, and President Eisenhower shortly afterward upped this number to 2,200.

This was a nice round figure and certainly should have been because it was so well padded. Both Mr. Brownell and President Eisenhower were reluctant to give a breakdown on it, but finally broke down enough to admit what the Washington newspapermen had already discovered for themselves—that this interesting number included people who had resigned in the normal turn-

"Gosh, It Isn't Even Safe To Resign Any More"

1/19/1954

over of government employees.

The reporters found out that the magic numbers included government employees who had merely transferred from one depart-

"Heart Attack, Poor Chap. Send Flowers And List Him As A Security Risk"

10/18/1954

ment to another, people who had left the government without even knowing they were under investigation—if they *were* being investigated—employees who had been hired and then fired by the current Administration, and a few dead people. The latter possibly illustrated the spiritual qualities that some government officials have spoken about so frequently. As a member of the Abou-ben-Adhem school of thought I could do with a little less public praying by politicians and a little more concern for the careers, the reputations and the lives that have been wrecked in the numbers racket.

One of the reasons for dismissals which was darkly and vaguely hinted at by Mr. Brownell was that some employees had committed past indiscretions which might make them subject to blackmail. There are certainly cases where possible blackmail might be a consideration, and the current officials were not the first to take this into account. But since there is no one who would like to relive every private moment of his life in public, this cause for dismissal can be widely abused and can itself become a kind of blackmail against worthy employees that politicians want to ease out.

Government employees—or any employees—are less subject to blackmail if they know that as long as they do their work loyally and conscientiously their employers will stand by them. And it seemed to me that pious talk on this subject might have been more impressive if it had come from an Administration which had not itself submitted to and encouraged blackmail by the worst elements in American politics. In appointing political blackmailers or in allowing them to move in on the executive branch, many people who claimed to be fighting subversion of government were in fact subverting it themselves.

There were two arguments advanced for the political numbers game. One was that by appearing to show that a lot of Communists were being cleaned out, the politicians were "restoring confidence in government," and should be praised for this performance. Since many of the people who were "restoring confidence" in government were the same ones who had worked so long and hard to destroy confidence in it, this would have been a good deal like praising a racketeer who had smashed store windows for "restoring order" after he had forced his victims to give him a cut of the business. There was always a very simple way to restore confidence, and that was by giving an honest accounting of what Communists—if any at all—the new Administration had actually found in government. This would be an obvious solution for men who were more interested in restoring faith in the government than they were in destroying faith in the opposition party.

The other argument was that government officials who played the numbers game and whipped up their own scares about Communism were "taking the ball away from McCarthy"—which was about as sensible as if our government, in the thirties, had embraced anti-Semitism and plunked for Nazi imperialism to "take the ball away" from Hitler.

It doesn't take much knowledge of numbers to know that you don't diminish things by adding and multiplying. Reckless charges and unwarranted fears are decreased only by exposing them for what they are. In our U. S. Information Program abroad we have long maintained that Truth Is a Weapon. It's a good weapon at home too, for those who are willing to use it.

The politicians continued onward and upward with the security-risk figures, and when one number fell out from under them they jumped to a higher one. Security figures in Washington shot up faster than those on the New York Stock Exchange. By March 1954, Vice President Nixon was telling a nationwide TV audience that 2,400 people had left the government under the security program. It was in this same speech that Mr. Nixon said, in praise of Secretary Dulles—and in obvious derogation of men like Cordell Hull, George C. Marshall and Dean Acheson—"Isn't it wonderful, finally, to have a Secretary of State who is not taken in by the Communists?" I thought it was fine that we had in the United States so many people who not only weren't taken in by Communism but who also weren't taken in by McCarthyism, even when it wore a Dickey front.

When President Eisenhower, in his 1955 State of the Union message, made only a modest one-line reference to the "improved security system," he neglected to mention how improved it really was. From a political standpoint it had improved almost fourfold in little more than a year. The latest figure was 8,008. An

"Ah, Yes—Isn't That Fellow McCarthy Terrible?"

7/2/1954

"Here He Comes Now"

10/29/1954, on the Nixon 1954 campaign trip

"I Think We've Been Had"

3/17/1954

editorial in *The Washington Post and Times Herald* pointed out that this 8,008 number had the particular virtue of looking the same if you read it either sitting upright or standing on your head, and that it meant just as much either way. I thought it was better viewed from the standing-on-the-head position, because this seemed the appropriate way to look at the entire program.

John Cramer, who writes the Federal employee news column for *The Washington Daily News,* said in late 1954 that employees *hired* by the Administration and later released might account for as high as 75 per cent of the total. Mr. Cramer's figures may even have been on the conservative side. Testifying in April 1955 before a Government Operations Subcommittee, Fred Ayer, Air Force intelligence representative, said that "95 per cent of the Air Force statistics" publicized as security-risk cases "would be probationary employees"—that is, people with less than one year's service. And he said the same system of reporting such people to the Civil Service as "security-risk separations" was still in use in the government.

In the same 1955 message in which he made his brief reference to the "improved security program," President Eisenhower said, "We shall continue to ferret out and destroy Communist subversion in government." He did not say what Communist subversion had been found—if any—or under what Administration these Communist subversives—if any—had been hired. And the best ferreting job in town still seemed to have been done by the many able newspaper correspondents who had dug out the secrets of the security-risk system itself. But whatever it was that the politicians were doing, they undoubtedly intended to keep on doing it, and with more and bigger numbers.

PERJURED
GOVT. TESTIMONY

2/22/1955

4. CAME THE DAWN

A SPECIAL characteristic of the early silent movies was their deadly determination that nobody should be left behind on any transition in the film. This they managed with the aid of the Everlasting Subtitle, which left nothing in doubt except possibly why the picture had been made at all.

When one of those Came-the-Dawn lines filled the screen, it stayed there till it sank in. Above the crackle of peanut shells and the tinny trills of the piano you could hear the couple behind you reading it aloud for their own edification, then passing it along to Junior and, a little louder, to Grandpa, who didn't hear too well even when he wasn't winding his watch. In hardly more than a minute the word was all around the theater that dawn had come. And then, as a clincher, there appeared on the screen an actual picture of the sun peeping up, with maybe the heroine shading her eyes and pointing to it.

It may not have come up like thunder, but it came unmistakably and with proper notice. Nobody had to ask anyone on the way out.

If the turns of public affairs were as clearly defined it would save a lot of confusion. But in national trends we're seldom certain at what precise point the darkness began moving in, or moving back. Nobody knew exactly when the Great Depression of the thirties ended, and it would be hard to say when the Great Mental Depression of the fifties slowly started to lift. But some time during 1954 or early 1955 the realization began to break through that every other guy couldn't be a sneaking subversive, and that there was something screwy about a lot of this security stuff.

One turning point may have been the Radulovich case, which was brought to the attention of televiewers by Edward R. Murrow.

"My Mother Is More Patriotic Than Your Mother"

8/9/1955

Air Force Lieutenant Milo Radulovich, whose loyalty was not even questioned, was being ousted from the armed forces for being guilty of association with his father—who was suspected

**"And If I May Say So,
I've Never Been Good
To My Mother"**

8/19/1955

"Er—How Do You Do"

9/2/1955

of reading un-American or non-American periodicals—and with a married sister, who was accused of having been a picket in a pro-Communist demonstration. In a country where blood runs thicker than official ink, the national reaction was much like that of the Radulovich neighbors. The government was throwing this boy out because he refused to disown his father and sister? *Huh?*

By the time the young lieutenant was reinstated a lot of people had become aware not only that strange things were being done in the name of security but that these things affected more than some faceless "bureaucrats" in Washington. If such a thing could happen to that young officer in Michigan, it could happen also to somebody in your neighborhood, or in your family.

Another turning point may have been the Ladejinsky case, which illustrated the madness in the methods which the government was using.

Certainly the Senate's condemnation of McCarthy, following the report of the Watkins Committee, marked a change.

But future researchers interested in turns will have a hard time finding anything giddier than the revolving activities of whirling Harvey Matusow, or anything better illustrating the dizziness of the security snafu.

Mr. Matusow, who had been a Communist for a couple of years, having joined in 1947 when he was about twenty years old, is a former informer-performer. He had been one of those professional witnesses who "have testimony, will travel," and who apparently was ready on almost no notice at all to identify almost anybody as a Communist at fifty paces. To augment his income he performed in night clubs as well as in Congressional hearing rooms, courts, and political campaigns.

Early in 1955 he declared publicly that his testimony as a hired witness had been false and that he had lied about some 245 people in Congressional inquiries alone.

This news was received with pain by the committees before which Matusow had testified, and by the Department of Justice, which had not only used his testimony in court but had kept him on its payroll. They seemed distressed not because injustices had been done but because Mr. Matusow had embarrassed them.

**"Beat It—We've Got
An Election To Win"**

10/12/1954

**"You Disloyal American!
You Communist!"**

4/12/1954

"This Could Spoil The Whole Racket, Men"

2/2/1955

They had helped to publicize him, they had bought his wares—
with the taxpayer's money, true, but good hard cash neverthe-

less—and now he had turned on them. It was downright ungrateful of him.

In their anguish and sorrow they could not be expected to think things through too clearly, and the first reaction of some of these officials was to exclaim that Matusow had been a Communist all the time. But young Harvey had possibly gauged the changing climate better than his patrons. The cry of "Communist!" wasn't quite enough any more, particularly since in this case it was an explanation that explained nothing.

Perhaps he had made a complete turn of the merry-go-round and become a Communist again. Perhaps, as they asserted, he had been a Communist all the time. But these were the men who had billed themselves as red-hot investigators and Communist-hunters. These were the fellows who could spot a Communist that the ordinary eye could not detect. What had they been doing clutching a Communist to their collective bosom all this time—and so thoroughly failing to recognize him as one that they had been happy to take his word against hundreds of other Americans?

Whatever Matusow is or was, how could they have been gullible enough to have placed any credence in him anyhow? Any child with or without a Dick Tracy badge might well have questioned the ability of this money-seeking, publicity-seeking fringe character to recognize, as he had claimed, 10,000 Communist Party members in New York "by sight." And if they had known him for what he was, then the inescapable conclusion was that they had been more interested in prosecutions—or persecutions—than they were in justice.

The officials who had embraced Matusow were now somewhat in the position of the wrestler who became so entangled with his opponent that neither of them could move. Finally the wrestler's manager whispered, "Bite him in the leg!"—which the wrestler proceeded to do, and immediately let out a scream of pain because he had bitten his own leg. The red-faced "red-hunters" could now hardly open their mouths about Matusow without biting themselves.

A Senate committee, headed by Senator Eastland, summoned

CONGRESSIONAL INVESTIGATORS AND DEPT. OF JUSTICE OFFICIALS WHO ACCEPTED MATUSOW'S TESTIMONY

HERBLOCK
©1955 THE WASHINGTON POST CO.

"Exactly! There's A Plot To Make Us Look Foolish"
2/8/1955

Matusow to testify and accused him of being a champion liar. This he readily conceded, and pointed out that he had said it first. There then ensued a strange verbal tussle in which committee members accused Matusow of having been an honest man in his previous testimony, while Matusow staunchly defended his dishonor.

The second line of defense for those who felt let down by Matusow was that We Mustn't Lose Faith in Other Informers Just Because of This One. This sounded a little odd, coming from some who had been willing to suspect millions of people and condemn two Administrations and even an entire political party on the strength of the Hiss case.

Unfortunately for them, Matusow seemed to have started something of a trend. Officials who had previously enjoyed the sound of public breast-beating and the confession of political sin were now disturbed by the rumble of more breast-beating by some of the same people.

Mrs. Marie Natvig had been a witness for the Federal Communications Commission in a case against Edward Lamb, Ohio newspaper publisher, who was defending his license to operate radio and TV stations. Mrs. Natvig, in testifying for the FCC, had said that Lamb had Communist connections. She now said that her testimony had been false. The FCC, at this point, found her to be an improbable witness, a fact which was apparent to most observers much earlier.

Lowell Watson, another witness in the same case, had previously testified for the Immigration Commission and was a star witness in a current government deportation case. He stepped forward—or backward—to admit perjury in *his* testimony against Lamb. Other informers also joined the Turnabout Club.

An article on the Watson twice-turned tale revealed how informer-performers can "corroborate" one another. Murrey Marder, of *The Washington Post and Times Herald,* reported an interview which reveals a remarkable example of what might be called guilt-by-*non*association, as well as guilt-by-association-of-informers. To quote from Mr. Marder's report:

> Watson's story is that former Communist William Garfield Cummings, onetime FBI informant, told him he had been dropped as a "consultant" by the Justice Depart-

ment, but expected to be hired as an FCC investigator if the FCC was "successful" in the Lamb case.

At Cummings' urging, said Watson, he agreed to prepare a statement on Lamb. . . .

Cummings, he said, wanted him to say that Lamb was a "secret Communist." Watson said he replied he did not know that; he said Cummings replied that he was "convinced in my own mind that Ed Lamb was a secret Communist."

They started to talk about the meaning of the term, Watson said; Cummings asked him for a definition. He said he told Cummings it meant a person who does not appear on Communist membership rolls, pays no dues which are listed, and is never seen at Communist functions.

Said Watson: "He [Cummings] said, 'Well, doesn't that definition of yours fit Mr. Lamb pretty precisely?'"

"I said, 'It could fit a lot of people.'"

"He convinced me that it could conceivably fit Mr. Lamb," said Watson.

Watson has testified that Cummings edited portions of Watson's statement on Lamb, and then signed it as a witness. It succeeded in bringing Watson into the case—where Cummings testified as the first government witness.

Using this nifty system, anyone could be branded a "secret Communist"—and by two witnesses.

This would be funny if human lives and reputations were not at stake, and if the testimony of such men was not bought and paid for by agents of the United States Government.

As Mr. Marder pointed out, these were public cases in which there was at least the right of cross-examination. But what about the thousands of "security" cases in which the accused has no opportunity to face the accuser, in which the accuser, in fact, is not even known?

The third and final line of defense of the Former Friends of

"Let's Have A Look At Those Securities"

3/7/1955

Former Informer-Performers was that criticisms of security methods were attacks on the FBI, and that questioning the use of informers like Matusow was a subversive attempt to make it difficult for the FBI to carry on its work. If the last refuge of a scoundrel is patriotism, apparently the final inner sanctum of that refuge, for those who have made a racket of anti-Communism, is the FBI. This they apparently look upon as being above flag, above government, above country—and certainly above any possible criticism, which they seem to regard as something akin to coming out for the abolition of motherhood.

The vocal eagerness of these people to defend the FBI, or to use that agency in their defense, must have been received with

"I've Got A Little List, Too"

5/26/1955

"Boss, I Don't Think He Wants Me In There"

1/20/1955

mixed feelings by J. Edgar Hoover, who was noticeably quiet at this time. Mr. Brownell and Mr. Hoover did not make a joint television appearance to say whether or not the FBI had sent the Attorney General a memorandum of twenty-eight pages or any number of pages about Harvey Matusow, or any other of the informer-performers.

It should be added, of course, that no Congressional committee asked them. This indicated a remarkable lack of curiosity. What does the Department of Justice, which screens so many other people, do about screening the people on its own payroll, particularly paid witnesses? Do the shoemaker's children go barefoot? What are the standards for the Justice Department's own employees? Judging from some of the informers and former FBI agents who get into the public prints, there must be occasional slip-ups in the type of people employed—even as in other departments of government.

In one of his excellent books, *The Loyalty of Free Men,* Alan Barth pointed out that all government departments must be subject to questioning and scrutiny, and said, "It is not healthy in a democracy that any governmental agency—and least of all a police agency—should be considered above criticism." Certainly no investigation of security methods can be complete if it is shy about going into FBI reports and the use of professional witnesses.

During a two-year period, 1952-54, some eighty-seven informers and professional witnesses, technically known as "consultants," were paid salaries by the Department of Justice. In April 1955 Attorney General Brownell announced that his department had some months before abandoned the practice of retaining full-time "consultants" on communism at guaranteed salaries, but said that it would continue to pay fees to "expert witnesses."

At this writing neither the Department of Justice nor any of the Congressional committees has shown an inclination to do anything that might result in actions against their professional witnesses (other than those who had turned on them), although several of these have been publicly denounced as liars.

One of the rare instances in which the Justice Department imposed any penalty on one of its own people was when it fired

"All Right, Leo—That's Enough"

6/29/1955

one of its holdover prosecutors, William A. Gallagher. Mr. Gallagher had secured an indictment against former State Department economist Val Lorwin, but the Department of Justice finally had to withdraw the case, conceding that there was no evidence to support its charges.

According to Attorney General Brownell, Gallagher had "indicated that he had felt it was better to indict Lorwin on slight evidence rather than appear before a Senate committee to explain why he had not obtained an indictment." This, however, might not have occurred under an Attorney General who impressed upon his subordinates that the business of the Department of Justice is not politics but justice.

Gallagher was tossed out but Brownell said there was no occasion to prosecute him for malfeasance in office.

The Justice Department has, however, continued to prosecute people accused by questionable witnesses, and has done so with astonishing vigor. When Judge Luther Youngdahl threw out of court the department's vague charges against Owen Lattimore, U. S. Attorney Leo Rover made an unprecedented attack on the judge for being, as nearly as I could make out, prejudiced in favor of the Constitutional rights of American citizens; and Rover demanded that the judge withdraw from hearing the case.

Judge Youngdahl, who apparently does not like attempted intimidation of the courts any more than he likes unsubstantial charges, looked the threat in the eye and smacked it down. After the U. S. Court of Appeals had twice upheld Judge Youngdahl, Attorney General Brownell finally gave up and dropped the Lattimore case.

For Mr. Brownell it seemed to be one of those years when just everything goes wrong.

In the "loyalty" case of Dr. John P. Peters, which involved the entire security program by challenging the use of anonymous informers, U. S. Solicitor General Simon Soboloff, a man of great ability and integrity, declined to argue the Justice Department's case before the U. S. Supreme Court.

But perhaps the unkindest cuts of all came from those to whom the Administration might have felt it could look for support of its methods.

Most surprising was the "Cain Mutiny" of the ex-senator who had been a member of the Jenner-McCarthy wing of the Republican party and who was, after his defeat for re-election, appointed by President Eisenhower to the Subversive Activities Control Board.

Traveling Papers

6/24/1955

In a series of speeches former Senator Harry Cain called for an overhaul of the entire security program and the liquidation of the Attorney General's subversive list, which he described as "a heinous thing" and which at that point had reached a total of 282 organizations. Pointing out one way in which this list is used—or, rather, misused—he cited a question in a printed form which at that time was being used by the Defense Department in its Industrial Security Program:

> Are you now associating with, or have you in the past five years associated with any individuals, including relatives, who you know or have reason to believe are, or have been, members of any organizations designated by the Attorney General . . .

A person could wind up in the jug for making a mistake in answering a question like that. But more than that, Mr. Cain pointed out, "We are not accustomed to any citizens' informer system in this country. Yet throughout defense plants in America we have established one. . . ."

What we have also established has been a kind of governmental Gresham's law by which counterfeit patriots have been driving real ones out of circulation.

This fairy-tale type of security recalls the story of "The Emperor's New Clothes," in which charlatans pretended to weave the emperor's garments of a wonderful material visible only to worthy people. So, as you remember, everyone pretended to see the invisible garments, until a child in the crowd watching the emperor parade down the street spoke up to say, "But he has no clothes on!"

There's been quite a weaving job done in our country the past few years. The weavers have told us they were making a wonderful security fabric, the latest thing—Communist-resistant, propaganda-proof, can be used for writing under water or under oath, with a belt in the back and maybe another one over the head. And anyone who fails to see the beauty of what they're doing is unpatriotic, or at the very least uncouth.

And for this phony protection they would strip us of our traditions of justice, of our Constitutional guarantees, of privacy and decency, and leave us in naked *in*security.

4/5/1953

5. THOSE MEN IN THE WHITE HOUSE

BACK IN the thirties there was a story about a man who went to the race track on his 55th birthday, traveled in car number 55, and found that his room in the hotel near the track was number 55. Knowing a red-hot hunch when he had one, he bet everything he had on the fifth horse in the fifth race, a steed named Five-By-Five. He watched his horse break in front, increase its lead at the quarter, and stay ahead until the stretch, where it was nosed out just under the wire. The hunch bettor stared darkly at the finish line as he tore up his tickets and muttered, "Damn that man Roosevelt!"

For all I know that story may have gone to the post for the first time during the term of Jackson or Jefferson, or whenever Presidents and horses started running. It's been generally accepted that along with the official glory, the oversize Thanksgiving turkeys, the Indian feathers, livestock, and portraits made entirely from bits of old bottles, a President also gets a collection of cracks aimed at "that man in the White House." And if some people give him undeserved credit for everything including nice weather, there are others who blame him for early frost, scratched fenders and the noise from the apartment upstairs. These are all, in their ways, tributes to the power of the highest office and greatest pain-in-the-neck job within the gift of the people.

Anyone who doesn't fully appreciate the power of that office needs only to sit in on a White House press conference, or watch the parts that appear on television, and then look at the newspaper headlines the next day. The remarks that seemed to be dropped casually have sprouted into half a dozen Page One headlines; and commentators have put the Presidential words under a microscope to study them and interpret their precise meanings. A new President must sometimes look at the morning paper and think, "Gosh, did I do all that?"

"You Mean Little Ol' Me?"

1/10/1955

He does all that, and in a few minutes at a press conference. On the other hand, he has to spend a great deal of time on things he shouldn't have to cope with. When President Eisen-

"Now Knowland, Now Martin, Now Bridges And Nixon"
12/15/1953

hower was suddenly taken ill in Denver in late September 1955, there was an equally sudden flurry of articles about the burdens of the Presidency, which have been oppressive for many years and through several administrations. Our Chief Executives not only have to face momentous decisions, but are also expected to perform an unlimited number of ceremonial routines, in addition to receiving countless delegations, submitting to endless handshaking and—among minor incidental chores—signing their names about 200 times a day.

So I've never been able to work up a good mad about Presidential recreations. As far as I'm concerned, any President is entitled to relax in whatever way he likes, whether it's golf, swimming, quoits or curling—if he can find time for them between the burdens of office, patting children on the head in the Rose Garden, and receiving visitors who don't mind chopping up a President's time so that they can say they met the President. He can weave rag rugs for all I care, and I'll be happy to contribute a drawerful of old socks.

I think the only time the irony entered my soul on official recreations was in 1953 when high officials were bragging about having eliminated "coffee breaks" for the rank-and-file employees. I mentioned in a talk at the time that there were no coffee breaks for the hard-working political higher-ups who were out plodding around on the hot golf courses. But this was aimed less at their fondness for the fairways than at their attempts to make bums out of all the other government employees who also work better for an occasional break in the routine.

It seems to me that the only criterion for judging officials is how they do their work. I was never bothered about President Truman's strolling around the Florida keys in sport shirts, nor by President Eisenhower's golfing, which provided material for a number of lighthearted drawings. So have all Presidential recreations—including Coolidge's mechanical horse, which in quieter days kept trotting into cartoons for months.

I haven't been one to snarl and swear about "that man in the White House." In fact, it was my modest complaint—and one not meant in any physical sense—that President Eisenhower too often had *not* been that man in the White House.

Despite all the good will flowing to and from the White House, a President—whatever his previous occupation—is in politics. He

3/27/1955, on the deportation of squirrels from the White House lawn.

is the leader of his party. And if he is a "prisoner of the White House," he is also the warden of his administration and the man whose word is absolute among his subordinates.

In referring to Mr. Eisenhower as not having been "that man in the White House," I mean that he didn't seem to me to have exercised the full responsibility of the office. From a political standpoint it's understandable that his advisers have always wanted to keep him above or apart from the kind of hassles and decisions that are bound to leave some people disgruntled. But with public officials popularity is something like money. And as people are always saying about money, it's not something to be valued for itself alone but for what you can *do* with it. Some of it may have to be spent for necessities; and sometimes, by investing in worth-while things, the capital can even be increased. You can't take it with you, because the history books may have a different way of toting accounts.

The popularity of President Eisenhower has certainly remained at a high level. This phenomenon has been so remarkable that it's caused some commentators to give up political analysis and go in for psychoanalysis. It used to be, in simpler days, that George Washington was the father of his country and that was that. But now any President of unusual popularity is referred to as a "father image."

If we're going to get into psychopolitical stuff, I want to play too, because I know just as little about psychiatry as the rest of the boys who bandy the terms about. The way I see it, fellows, President Eisenhower is more what you might call an "uncle image," a technical term that came to me one day while drawing a picture of Uncle Sam and wishing I was lying down on a couch.

Papa is a guy who has to cope with a lot of little day-in-and-day-out problems of running a family. He has to double in housework and help the kids with their homework. Papa is expected to know the answers to all questions; and if he's not also *au courant* with everything the kids are familiar with, he's likely to be regarded as something of a square. Papa has to keep the kids' taffy out of the neighbors' hair, repair the furnace, fix the busted bicycle, decide who'll drive the car, keep an eye on everything and see that the kids don't get out of line. Papa sometimes has to get mad and say, "Hey, I told you to *stop!*"

**"I'll Compromise
And Make The Chain
A Little Longer"**

1/9/1954

**"Let's See—
What'll I Look
Into Next?"**

4/12/1953

But Uncle is a regular guy and everybody likes him—although with all his charm and glamour he's not quite so close to us and our little problems as Papa is. Eisenhower seems to me to be like a favorite uncle who won fame and fortune abroad and whose every appearance is a treat. He has only to pop his head in the door and smile to make the kids feel that this is kind of a special occasion and some of the old family regulations are going to be relaxed.

Uncle buys the kids pistols and popcorn and takes them to the ball game. Discipline, routine, education and explanations are not among the responsibilities of unclehood. And when it's time for some of the more irrepressible youngsters to stop chalking up the walls and carving up the carpets, Uncle will still be smiling and waving to them as the little tykes are carried—kicking, clawing and screaming—to their little beds.

Roosevelt seemed more like Papa and, judging by the criticism he got, perhaps he was. With all the attacks that were made on him I can't remember anyone ever having said, "You shouldn't blame him because, after all, he doesn't know what's going on in his Administration." If a fellow's going to play Papa in a national *Life with Father,* he's got to *know.*

Anyhow, Ike is Uncle, and the political wiseacres can't tell me different. He may even be Uncle Sam himself, minus the chin whiskers—a national symbol personified, and one which takes the place of the kings and queens and princesses that so many Americans secretly long for.

But I think a President has to provide leadership in more than a symbolic sense, and must at least ride herd on his own official family. From the way people have talked about "the men around the President" you'd think he was being hustled off by a riot squad. After all, there's nobody around him that he doesn't want there, and there's no use having to strain himself to protect us from people he puts there.

In 1953 the American Telephone and Telegraph Company presented the President with the fifty-millionth telephone in the U. S.—a special job trimmed with 48 gold stars. It would not be a bad idea to have embossed on that phone in gold letters the

"What Does He Think We Are—Legislators?"

1/15/1954

first complete sentence spoken over the instrument when Alexander Graham Bell said to an assistant in another room, "Mr. Watson, come here. I want you."

TRADE
PROGRAM

HERBLOCK
©1955 THE WASHINGTON POST CO.

"Fireman, Save My Child"

3/21/1955

Forty-nine million other phones might well bear the words "Tempus Fugit" or, in some homes, "Use Only in Case of Emergency." But for a President, the words of Mr. Bell would be a

constant reminder that he's the head man and that he has only
to pick up the receiver to say, "Mr. Brownell" or "Mr. Dulles" or
Mr. anybody—"Come here. I want you."

President Eisenhower has expressed many fine sentiments, but
he may well suffer from a habit similar to one I'm afflicted with.
This is the business of making a list of things to be done, feeling
a sense of some accomplishment at having written them out, and
then stuffing the list into my coat pocket, where it will rub
against previous lists filed there until the penciled notations are
no longer legible. When I do that the only consequences may
be that the laundry doesn't get picked up or that the vacuum
cleaner doesn't get fixed. But a President's plans are something

"It's Not Customary, Mr. Wilson"
1/22/1953

"Look—Why Not Take A Penalty Stroke And Get Back On The Fairway?"

4/22/1955

else again. He can't just set down well-intentioned words and let it go at that. He has to follow through.

Sometimes even when a program is outlined and supposedly put into effect, it doesn't take hold if the right people aren't administering it. In government you can't tell the program without the players.

A case in point was the naming of John B. Hollister, a former Taft aide and executive director of the second Hoover Commission, to be in charge of all the foreign-aid programs. When asked about this appointment, the President confessed that he didn't know if Mr. Hollister was in sympathy with our foreign-aid efforts. Mr. Hollister himself didn't know how he stood on the current program, and there was an awkward pause of several days while he studied it. On a thing like that, I'd think the President might have found some way to have the appointee sounded out about his views before naming him.

"When Do We Sail, Cap'n?"

2/16/1955

Rugged Individualism

2/28/1955

Unless the Number 1 man keeps a close watch on the team, the individual players are likely to call their own individual signals and get to running into one another, as, in fact, they often have. And his policies are likely to seem like the Cheshire cat in *Alice in Wonderland* at the point where it was just a big smile, fading out into nothingness.

Some of the team members appear in these drawings, where they are generally shown in less than their finest hours. I don't like to belabor the team, and would prefer to be more often in the cheering section. But I found early in the game that there are hazards in cheering this team too soon. Every once in a while the captain or one of the leaders will take a fine position that makes me feel like letting out a "Yea, team!" But then things get confused by a series of clarifying statements, explaining that the position isn't quite what it seemed.

When you think the team has taken a good firm stand on something, there's nothing more embarrassing than getting in the middle of a long cheer and suddenly finding that they've executed the maneuver known as getting the hell out of there.

Sometimes the course is changed as a result of a wet finger held aloft revealing that it might be expedient to operate differently. The Administration people aren't the only ones who watch the polls; a lot of Democrats in Congress have restrained themselves from what they felt was needed criticism of the executive department because they had been impressed by Presidential popularity polls. There are poll parrots in both parties. But important decisions can't be made on the basis of polls alone. If they could, we might as well turn over all policy-making functions to Mr. Gallup. Leaders need to have definite ideas about what's necessary; and a President, as national leader, party leader and symbol before the world, has to be ready to go to bat for convictions about things that are important.

A President, as White House correspondent Merriman Smith observed in the title of one of his books, is many men. There was a time, during the Hoover Administration, when one might have supposed this to be literally so. Callers used to keep emerging from the executive offices in those days, announcing that "There's a new Hoover in the White House," until you'd have thought the Hoovers were rolling off an assembly line. Perhaps they were because they all seemed very much alike, and the model does

"Who's Ahead In The Defense Department?"

6/22/1954

**"Come In, Ezra—
How's The
Weather Out There?"**

1/14/1954

82

"I Can Be Flexible"

8/17/1954

**"Let's See —
New Zealand,
Thailand, Knowland—"**

4/16/1954

not seem to have changed much, even after more than a quarter of a century.

Certainly a President seems like many different men to many different people, each of whom has his own ideas of what a President should be and of what he actually is. And a mythology is built up around every President, whether he likes it or not. It may have a basis in fact, or it may be made up of labels that political opponents and his own public relations men have stuck on him. Sometimes it takes years for these to wear off before we can see what he was actually like.

A friend of mine, when dissatisfied with any Administration, used to grumble that the people never got what they expected

"Yoo Hoo—Charlie"
10/13/1954

"What Was Wrong With Charlie's Crack About Dogs?"
10/14/1954

in a President. It was his contention that if we elected a man to keep us out of war, we got into war; that when we elected a Great Humanitarian, people went hungry; and so on. Of course, nobody knows what prompts each voter to mark his X for a candidate, so it would be hard to say who expected what. But the last couple of Administrations offer some interesting paradoxes anyhow.

President Truman received his share of criticism from many of us when we thought it necessary, and more than his share from others when it was not necessary. He has generally been described as a "politician," sometimes in the sense of the word which suggests a man primarily interested in elections and patronage. The record of this politician is quite interesting.

He appointed many Republicans to high offices.

For a man with comparatively little previous experience in

"We're Off!"

3/30/1954

"Well, How Much Have We Got Left Today?"

8/4/1953

world affairs he did quite well abroad with things like the
Marshall Plan, the Truman Doctrine, the Point 4 Program, NATO,
etc.—although he was regarded by some as a wastrel because he

"I'm Getting A Little Tired Of This Honeymoon"

6/23/1953

extended so much aid to people who did so little voting in American elections. His foreign policies were, in fact, good enough for the succeeding Administration to get back to most of them, even though it did so on tippy-toe.

"Fine! Fine! Maybe You'll Do Better Next Time"

8/31/1954

"Thanks For Your Cooperation"

7/1/1955

"Couldn't You Sometime Lock The Door *First?*"

3/25/1955

He stood up for civil rights and lost the Solid South.

In such actions as his vetoes of the McCarran Acts he spoke up for civil liberties and found himself attacked as being "soft on Communists."

Long, Long Trail

7/15/1955

He stood up to Communist aggression abroad and was politically clobbered for "sending our boys to die in Korea."

For a fellow who was supposed to be "just a politician," this
devotion to principle without regard to political price tags or

"It Must Be Nice
To Be A Friend
Of The President"

7/23/1954

"Atomic Energy? Sure.
Just A Minute Now—"

2/11/1955

"And They Used To Say I Was Stubborn"

2/6/1955

popularity polls was quite a remarkable performance. And if all
that was "politics," I think it was a pretty good kind of politics
to have in a President of the United States. Whether or not one
agreed with all his policies, it can hardly be said that his sense
of politics outran his sense of duty.

"Okay, Now Give Us That Old Smile"

11/2/1953

It may also be contrary to popular impressions, but it seems to me there's been much more partisanship in the Administration that followed Mr. Truman's, despite the fact that President Eisenhower did not come to the office as a party politician. This is not to say that Mr. Eisenhower has consciously tried·to provide

**"You Know,
That Piano Playing
Wasn't So Bad"**

2/22/1953

**"Truman
Just Gave A Little
Back-Platform Talk"**

10/2/1952

"Official Statement—Politics Is Not Interfering With Our Work—"

11/14/1954

an extremely partisan Administration. The nonpolitician may lean heavily on others for political advice, just as a nonmilitary man might give greater weight to the advice of military experts than would a soldier-President.

In any case, almost no members of the opposition party have

"Now, See That Nobody Gets Into These Peanuts"
10/28/1954

been appointed to high office in this Administration. Politics was brought into the civil service with a White House order directing party members to clear career-job applications with the party's National Committee. It was brought into the Atomic Energy Commission, where, as David Lilienthal pointed out, Mr. Truman had made appointments without even inquiring about political affiliations. The current Administration condoned the most sweeping attacks against the opposition party; and politics was played with the internal security system.

These policies may have been due to those men around the President that we keep hearing about. If we feel strongly about such things, I suppose we can say, "Oh, those men in the White House!" or "Darn those men around the man in the White

"You Sure That Cloud Will Hold Both Of Us?"

8/1/1955

House!" or "Drat those men under the men around the man in the White House!"

Those are unwieldy phrases. They don't have any zing in them, and people aren't going to use them. If responsibility continues to get kicked around till it's lost—or passed around till it's

"Sweetest Little Feller—Everybody Knows—"

1/14/1955

hidden, like a game of "Button, button, who's got the button?"—
this is likely to destroy a great national tradition; and we may be
reduced to crying "Who? Who?" like a flock of owls.

It's not what we've been accustomed to all these years. Somebody has to be responsible. Somebody has to know. Somebody

"Confidentially, He Hates It"

9/8/1955

has to say, "We'll do this, fellows" and "We'll stop that." Somebody has to say, "Sure I did it, and what about it?" Somebody has to be "that man in the White House."

Who ever heard of a political cartoon titled "What Are You

The Mountains Around Denver

9/27/1955

Going To Do About This, You Fellows Around And In And
Out Of The White House?" It sounds awful and it wouldn't
even fit the space. The time-honored line is "What About This,
Mr. President?"

Nothing Exceeds Like Excess

9/12/1952

6. PERSONA AU GRATIN

"MARLEY," began Charles Dickens in his most famous story, "was dead, to begin with."

I cite this not as a prelude to a jolly holiday tale or even to a Congress Carol, but merely to show that a statement like that doesn't necessarily end anything—not even when, as Dickens affirmed a moment later, "Old Marley was dead as a door-nail."

It may be that nothing, including a nail from the Senate Door, is as dead as yesterday's demagogue, wrapped up in yesterday's newspaper headlines. Still, a visit with Marley—transparent and horrible—was worth while; and it might be profitable to spare a few moments for another once lively subject in a similar condition.

To anyone who says, "Who's McCarthy? He's nothing!" I can only reply that I agree, and then ask why it was that this nothing occupied a nation for nearly five years and dominated almost half of a four-year Administration of his own party. Enough time has now passed since the surfeit of stories about him for us to be able to mention again, without reaching for a stomach remedy, the subject that was for so long Topic A.

During 1953 and 1954, suggestions kept coming in urging me to get out a book of the cartoons I'd drawn on this theme. But I didn't do it. This may have been partly because I begrudged him a book, but it was mostly because I didn't want to treat him as an isolated phenomenon, embodying in one person all the troubles that afflicted us. I'm happy now to put him more or less in solitary confinement in this chapter, but only to show that the "security" madness, the political immorality and the know-nothingism dealt with elsewhere in these pages did not begin or end with one character ostensibly in search of a plot.

The sickness of the times is still with us. And even if his song of hate is ended, the malady lingers on.

"Steady Now, Pal—
Don't Hamstring Me
In My Work"

2/25/1953

The New Broom

2/26/1953

104

"Harold, We've Got To Throw You To The Sheep"

3/12/1953

No demagogue is an island of mud unto himself, and this one didn't exist without solid connections with the political mainland. If he were completely finished, there would still be others

"We Have
Documentary Evidence
That This Man
Is Planning
A Trip To Moscow"

3/25/1953

"We Killed 'Em
In Europe, Boss"

4/23/1953

106

of his kind—and there will be more to come. They may lack the ingenuity to dramatize the case of an Army dentist as if he had been drilling away the very foundations of the nation. But they will have other gimmicks, and they will be helped along the way by some of the same sort of people who helped this one.

That's why I want to toss in a few words about his period of power, along with these cartoons which pick up his career in 1952. I'm not trying to lay a ghost but to dispel a few shadows.

The rise and fall of McCarthy might be summed up in a series of clichés:

"He's getting in there and digging Communists out of government, and that's the important thing."

"He may be going too far, but he woke the country to the Communist danger, and he's done more good than harm."

"Of course I don't like his methods, but I approve his objectives."

"Sure he's a phony, but he was built up by all that editorial criticism of him."

"I don't like him either and always said that some day he'd get his comeuppance."

Taking these disordered ideas in order:

The charges which he originated against alleged Communists in government set off a five-year wild-goose chase which produced a final score of one goose egg. The Eisenhower Administration in 1955 concluded its own investigations of people listed in his original charges and found not a single Communist.

Long before 1950, when the McCarthy era began, the country was so jittery about Communists at home that it welcomed the Truman loyalty-security program of 1947; and after the Hiss case disclosures in 1948, relating to events of several years before, there was considerable fear that perhaps even such methods and policies were not "tough" enough.

As for the McCarthy objectives, even aside from the fact that the end doesn't justify the means, his aims were never any better than his methods. The objective was clearly the achievement of personal power and the advancement of one man; and at no time was he doing more good than harm, or anything *but* harm.

OFFICIAL
STATE DEPARTMENT
—
PATRONIZE NO OTHER
—
DOCUMENTS
WHILE YOU WAIT
—
ALSO AVAILABLE FOR
PRIVATE EYE WORK,
PAMPHLETS, CRAP GAMES
AND GREASE JOBS
ALL WORK CONFIDENTIAL

HERBLOCK
©1953 THE WASHINGTON POST CO.

4/1/1953

It always seemed to me that even his adversaries did him an unwitting favor by taking him and others of his kind at their own valuation and referring to them as enemies of Communism

"Quick, Men—Get That Bible Off The Shelves"

7/7/1953

or red-hunters. As one commentator observed, such characters might better be called "head-hunters."

McCarthy was willing to accept Communist support when he

"I Want You To Shake Hands With— Say, What's Wrong With You Guys Anyhow

7/10/1953

Book Burns Man

7/17/1953

110

first ran for the Senate, and there was never anything to indicate that opportunists of his type — who had already adopted the methods of the Communists—would not have embraced Communism itself if it had really been going anywhere in our country.

As for the McCarthy build-up, there is no question that this junior Caesar fed upon publicity. But those who complained about the editorial criticisms of him showed a curious tendency to confuse the remedy with the disease. Their theory seemed to be that if he met no opposition this would spoil all his fun, and he'd give up to go home and sulk.

McCarthy in his heyday was a publicity genius who played the newspapers like a series of drums, beating out his primitive themes. His accusations got front-page play in headlines as bold as the senator himself. And he even had the effrontery to complain to—and threaten—newspapers which did not give him the publicity support to which he had become accustomed. Many conscientious newspapers found themselves reporting his crooked charges with a straight face because their standards of objectivity required them to give space to a United States senator who manufactured news. In these circumstances, for those papers which opposed him to have withheld editorial fire would have been to give his propaganda an almost clear field.

This brings us to the matter of McCarthy's too long delayed comeuppance and a few myths that need to be batted down before they get out of hand.

Rationalization is a powerful and dangerous sedative. After a tough fight everyone likes to think that what he did was exactly the right thing. Those who joined in at the kill feel they appeared at just the right time. And those who didn't join in at all can come out from under the beds afterward to say, "You see, it's just as I said. There never was anything to be alarmed about."

If there are enough of these, the people who bore the brunt of the battle may find themselves bearing the brunt of the post-mortems as well, this time being attacked for having been premature, or *too* militant.

I don't mind a guy coming late to meeting, and don't care too much if he tries to kid himself that everybody else arrived

"I Didn't Really Want To Blow Your House In, Anyhow"
12/10/1953

too early; but when he goes around making insulting remarks to all those who got there on time I get a little sore.

After the Watkins Committee recommendation to censure McCarthy, *Time* magazine hailed the work of the six senators for

"...kay, Bud.
...hen I Want You Again
...ll Send For You"

2/25/1954

"And I'd Still Like
To See You
Become President"

2/26/1954

113

"Have A Care, Sir"

3/4/1954

finding the "remedy" which, it said, "hysterical anti-McCarthyites had never found." I never found out what a "hysterical anti-McCarthyite" was, but presumably this was meant to apply to anyone who had called for action before the autumn of 1954.

The fact is that McCarthy's fraud was apparent from the start, and the case against him had always been well documented. Since the spring of 1950 no time was too early to speak up about him, and there was no time when colleagues in his party or in the Senate could not have smacked him down.

In 1950 Senator Margaret Chase Smith had offered a party "declaration of conscience" and found only six senatorial takers on her side of the aisle. The Tydings subcommittee had found McCarthy's charges baseless in the same year. Senator William Benton had brought charges which resulted in a Senate investi-

"Quick, Officer—They Went That Way"
4/27/1954

gation of McCarthy in 1951. When Senator Flanders forced the issue in 1954, senators even then had to be almost lassoed to face the situation.

There was no basic change in McCarthy between 1950 and 1954. He had taken to attacking Republicans as well as Democrats. And "hysterical anti-McCarthyites" had exercised enough effective counter-pressure to put public officials on the spot. But his methods were no different and his charges no more unsubstantial than they had been nearly five years before. His swipes at President Eisenhower were more gentle and cautious than his

"Beat It. We're Getting Material For McCarthy"
5/11/1954

"I Have Here In My Hand—"

5/7/1954

vicious attacks on another great general, George C. Marshall. His contempt of the Senate Subcommittee on Privileges and Elections, which was one of the principal bases of the Watkins Committee report, had occurred in 1951. No one had to wait four or five years or do any mystic divining to know what this character was like. There was nothing secret about the fact that the way to deal with him was to stand up to him and to condemn his actions.

For all the talk about McCarthy being a political lone wolf, he was never really alone and couldn't have achieved his peculiar success alone. What sustained him was not so much his gullible followers and fellow-traveling demagogues as the tacit support of "respectable" people who found it advantageous to go along with him, or at least to look the other way. They were the ones who kept him going.

Some were afraid to cross him and some hoped to reap political profit from his activities. McCarthy corrupted countless conservatives by offering a temptation they could not resist—a dirty stick with which to beat their political opponents. They did not even have to use it themselves. He and his friends would do the work for them; they merely had to remain silent.

And it was only when this McFrankenstein monster threatened to destroy his patrons that they became worried about him. There was then some indignation, but it was not moral indignation.

It's not pleasant to think that many "nice people" shared a responsibility for this kind of political gangsterism. It's more comfortable to feel that they had some shrewd strategy which eventually succeeded in bringing McCarthy to book. Unfortunately, the only high strategy was that which was all too painfully revealed at the so-called McArmy hearings, when it became obvious that Secretary of the Army Stevens had dutifully followed the team policy of appeasement and co-operation with the McCarthy gang.

This policy was probably best described in an October 1954 article in *The Reporter* magazine, written by Martin Merson. Mr. Merson is a businessman who had come to Washington as consultant to the International Information Administration and assistant to his friend Dr. Robert L. Johnson, who was director of that program. In his article, which included in the closing paragraphs a *mea culpa* sentence stating that "despite my deep convictions,

5/20/1954

6/2/1954

I too had let myself be caught in the web of expediency and appeasement," Mr. Merson said, in part:

> In the weeks that followed I got an education in practical politics at the highest levels. It was a rich experience for me, full of impressions that are still vivid in my memory.
>
> I recall especially my first visit to the White House, the pride I felt in participating in a conference with some of the President's closest advisers, and the chill and anger in my bones when I realized that the powerful men assembled there had cast their unanimous vote, in a matter of great importance to the information program, for what was openly described as the most expedient solution.
>
> Sherman Adams, the President's Special Assistant, who was presiding, pronounced the word "expediency" as if it meant nothing more than efficiency.
>
> Above all, I remember those men in government who felt that constant and public reiteration of high ideals had somehow earned them the right to practice the low arts of compromise and backstairs deals.

Everything comes out in the wash, but sometimes the laundry is a long time on the way. By the time McCarthy was toppled, at the end of 1954, most people were sick to death of him and of hearing about him. No time was wasted in gloating or indulging in recriminations. When the President wrote a note of congratulation to the Watkins Committee on its work, and when—after the vote of censure—it was announced that McCarthy was no longer on the White House guest list, nobody said, in the bitter words of Samuel Johnson to his patron, Lord Chesterfield, ". . . the notice which you have been pleased to take of my labors, had it been early, had it been kind; but it has been delayed till I am indifferent and cannot enjoy it. . . ."

It hasn't been my purpose to cry "Nyah! Nyah! Nyah!" here either. But memory can be almost as tricky as McCarthy, and I

"That's The Way It Looks, All Right"

6/8/1954

think it's important to keep the record straight.

After a danger has passed, it's surprising how easy it can be to forget that it ever existed. It was not long after World War II

**"I Pledge Allegiance To Joe McCarthy
And To The Committee Which Stands For Him—"**

6/17/1954

that we became so occupied with the threat of world Communism that many people seemed almost unable to remember that

High Noon In Washington

7/16/1954

war, or the Axis powers which forced it upon the world. It was, in fact, that very example of the nonpersistence of memory on

Pussyfootprints On The Sands Of Time

8/3/1954

which McCarthy capitalized after Russia had changed from war-time ally to cold-war enemy. It was this which enabled him to picture patriots as "traitors."

McCarthyism, too, will be discounted. Foreseeing this, Walter Lippmann wrote, on December 27, 1954:

A measure of how serious was the danger is how long it took, how difficult it was, to rally resistance. In the long months of timidity and vacillation damage was done to this country which it will take a very long time to repair. . . .

There is the damage to our self-respect and self-confidence. The effect has been not to shut off, but to damp down and in a degree to smother, the full exercise of the traditional American freedom of thought and of speech. There is a kind of smog in what should be the clean and open air of this free land, a smog which makes men nervous, makes them afraid to speak their minds, makes them not sure they dare keep their minds open.

There is the damage to the Government—to the morale, and indeed to the integrity, of the Foreign Service and of large portions of the Civil Service. Their injuries are subtle. But they are deep. It will take a long time to repair them. A decade would be a conservative estimate. . . .

And with all this, there is the damage to our reputation in the world. There, speaking the bitter truth, the promise of American life has been grossly tarnished by the virulent campaign of defamation against the whole history of an American generation. No one can measure what we have lost in influence and power by that campaign of self-defamation. But it is something that will not easily be made up by money and a multitude of bombs. . . .

. . . it is not, I believe, too optimistic to say that the conditions now exist in which we can begin the long task of repairing the damage that has been done to our unity and to our liberties. From now on, we can begin to recover the ground that in this free Nation should never have been lost.

"I Can't Do This To Me
9/14/1954

"Carry On, Lads"
10/7/1954

Still, Small Voice

11/30/1954

Because minor details are even more quickly forgotten, per-haps I should explain here the circumstances that prompted the cartoon of McCarthy and the two slings, which appeared the day after the Senate vote of censure. The debate on this issue had been postponed out of deference to McCarthy, who took himself to a hospital with what was said to be a bursitis condition in his arm. When he returned to the Senate, after an absence of twelve days, he carried his arm in a sling, and appeared thus when the Senate voted on him. It might be added that he was also something of a lame duck in another respect, being at that point about to lose his chairmanship of the Government Operations Committee as a result of the November 1954 election, in which the Senate went Democratic. This was a real blow to his power and possibly the decisive one.

I've devoted several pages here to a faded and frowsy subject because there are a few things I don't think we can afford to forget.

One of these days some youngster is going to pipe up, "Daddy, who *was* that fellow McCarthy anyhow, and what happened to him?" When that question is asked, I hope Daddy will not wrinkle his brow, pass an uncertain hand across it, and say, "Well, son, as I recall it, he was not much of a danger, but he was built up by criticism of him, and—let's see—he was finally cut down by a policy of letting him go the limit."

That would be untrue as well as uninspiring. A kid would do better to hang onto the Davy Crockett legends than to swap them for the myth that dangerous characters can be taken care of by sitting tight and doing nothing.

The McCarthy threat was not met by giving him enough rope to tie up the country and to hang everybody including himself. It was not met by people who regretted that nothing could be done about him because of the temper of the times. For those who don't want to speak up there is never a right time.

The threat was turned back by people who did something to change and improve the temper of the times; by people who were willing to stand up and fight back; by public officials like Senators William Benton and Herbert Lehman, who spoke up unequivocally, and Senator Ralph Flanders, who compelled a reluctant Senate to act. The challenge was faced by those witnesses before the McCarthy committee who refused to be in-

HERBLOCK
©1954 THE WASHINGTON POST Co.

12/3/1954

timidated; by those newspapers and commentators that would not be silent and refused to trim or hedge; and by people who, with-

"You Sure You Don't Want To Run Away From Home?"

12/12/1954

out benefit of public platforms or protective prestige, spoke up for themselves and for common decency as individual Americans.

They are the kind who did it. Since the earliest days of the

Little-Four Meeting
5/16/1955

country they are the kind who have always done it. That's what I think we need to remember.

Okay, now let the body be buried.

"Is There Somewhere Else To Go?"

11/18/1954

7. ROUND TRIP

WASHINGTON is like one of those early American ports, where stay-at-homes heard about faraway places and travelers swapped stories about experiences across the seas. But here it's all more casual than it was in those towns where people sang out about a sail on the horizon. A fellow is sorry to be late to a cocktail party because of a delay on a flight from Paris, or hates to leave early but has to be off for Ceylon. For a long time I've seemed to run into people who do intercontinental commuting with less fuss than I make about going downtown for a haircut.

After a few years of this I began to feel as if I'd spent my life in a broom closet, and when I finally got away for a quick trip to Europe I visualized the customs people on the other side looking over their lists, brushing their hands together and saying, "Well, that's the last of them. We've had 'em all now."

Actually, it turned out afterward that there were still a few others who 'hadn't been across yet, and it's been comforting to run into them because they're the only people who make me feel as if I've been anywhere. In most cases when people said they'd heard I'd been abroad, I'd open my mouth to tell them about it and hear a rush of words about Europe which turned out to be somebody else's. And I'd always be left with a lungful of air to be expended in short edgewise words like "Well, when I . . ." and "No, but I . . ." until the speaker and I both ran down.

They would interrupt themselves only to ask if I'd seen this or recalled that. And I never had. From what they told me I had missed everything worth seeing, and after a while I began to wonder if I'd been to Europe at all. I think they wondered too. They never put it in so many words, but their expressions sometimes asked if I was sure I hadn't got on the Hoboken ferry by mistake.

Apparently the only way a novice can get anyone to listen to his saga is to sign up with a psychiatrist, which hardly seems worth while from what I've heard about the going rates. What's really needed is an extra service in the tourist agencies, a professional listener who, for a modest fee, will smile and nod at the client's travelogue when he returns with his suitcase full of labels and his checkbook full of stubs.

After my post-travel experiences I was particularly interested in the televised White House meeting at which the Secretary of State reported to the President and other top officials about his 1955 trip to Austria. I was fascinated not by what Mr. Dulles had to say, but by the polite way everybody listened. It couldn't have been done without a rehearsal.

President Eisenhower acted as interlocutor, and every once in a while interjected a little remark like "They couldn't even build Rome in a day." He never let on that he'd been around quite a bit himself—and nobody else did either, including Vice President Nixon, who still must have had a few unused anecdotes about *his* trips abroad.

Secretary Dulles mentioned that the NATO council was a pretty stuffy and formalistic body, and that showed. that Mr. Dulles—or "Foster," as the President called him—was a real folksy fellow, even if it wasn't a diplomatic thing to say about his NATO colleagues.

It might be, as some commentators said, that the whole broadcast was more notable as a TV show than as an effort to inform the American people about the hard facts of world affairs, but it was certainly quite a performance and showed a great deal of politeness and courtesy all around. It wound up with the President thanking Mr. Dulles; and Mr. Dulles saying, "Well, it has been a great opportunity for me, Mr. President, to have this chance to tell you these things." There at the end I got the impression that if it hadn't been for the miracle of television, Mr. Dulles might never have got to tell the President about his trip at all. So maybe even an old traveler like Secretary Dulles has the same problem I had in getting the fellows to listen to his account of a trip.

"A Fellow Can't Remember To Take Everything"

9/19/1954

I've long since given up trying, and by now I'm not sure that
I want to talk about my trip at all. But for the benefit of those
readers who happen to be hopelessly trapped in caves with nothing but this book and a candle, I'll answer two brief questions.

"Pleased To Meet You, I Think"

10/5/1954

Did I return with any new ideas or convictions? Yes, I did. I came back firmly convinced of the desirability of lightweight luggage. The fellow who sold me my traveling bag explained that it was genuine six-ply brontosaurus skin, triple stitched to steel-girder reinforcements, and that it would last a lifetime. I'm sure it would, particularly if I kept on carrying it. But I want to last longer than the suitcase. So the next time I go out into the big wide world I'm going to carry my shirts in a valise made of cobwebs, preferably spun by the younger and more tender spiders. It won't wear like iron, but on the other hand—which happens to be mine—it won't feel like iron either; and I'll save enough in excess baggage charges on planes to lay in a lifetime supply.

The other question is: Did I meet any people abroad who seemed unfriendly? Yes, but only a few. These were some American tourists who were evidently trying hard to pass as natives. When I asked them please for directions, they reared back, horrified that I had recognized them as Americans and anxious to get away fast before they could be seen associating with a fellow countryman. All the rest, including Americans, were friendly and helpful as they could be.

I can't say that I got my fingers on the European public pulse because they—my fingers, that is, not the public—were too busy leafing through guidebooks. But I did see enough to illustrate how much we all have in common. For example, I got to the French National Assembly when the Premier (Laniel at the time) was delivering the equivalent of a State of the Union message. And, hearing a ripple run through the assembled deputies at one point, I turned to a British correspondent and asked what the Premier had just said.

"He said," interpreted my friend, "that there is too great a discrepancy between what the farmer gets for his produce and what the consumer has to pay for it." This rang a familiar gong, and I had the feeling that if the Parliament of Man is ever established, it's a safe bet that there'll be a line in the State of the World message about what the farmer gets and what the consumer pays. Suddenly the Assemblée Nationale was just like Capitol Hill. I had never left home.

In a way, I suppose none of us ever leaves home. Some of it

**"Hey—
What About The Man?"**

9/22/1954

"Friend Of Yours?"

1/28/1954

always goes with us. The departing tourist receives from his friends lists of things to buy for them, which—with a fair wind and some luck—can happen to blow overboard anywhere past Bedloe Island. He also receives, from the State Department, a pamphlet titled *Information for Bearers of Passports,* which tells him a lot of things he needs to know about the status of American citizens in certain countries.

This pamphlet begins with an excerpt from a speech by President Eisenhower on mutual understanding and friendship, which points out that we may occasionally be shocked by some opinions abroad that Americans are "immature diplomatically; impulsive, too proud of their strength, ready to fight, wanting war." He goes on to say that some people may consider Americans rude and may not even admire our deportment "because of unfortunate incidents on the part of individuals." "Each of us," he says, "whether bearing a commission from his Government or traveling by himself for pleasure or business, is a representative of the United States of America. . . ."

These are sound reminders, and if they're worth thinking about on an ocean voyage, they can also serve as a text for the remainder of this travel section. I could do no better than to pass these words back to Secretary Dulles, whose trips may not allow time for pamphlet reading, along with the added reminder that what our officials do at home *also* gives impressions of what we're like.

Anyone who regards the domestic work of the State Department as mere "housekeeping chores" forgets that those chores are performed in front of a picture window. The way our statesmen operate over here has its effects overseas; and I don't think statesmanship is likely to soar to great heights in the world if it's accustomed to covering the home grounds on its knees. Neither is it likely to cut a dashing figure while playing Sweet Alice to some senatorial Ben Bolt.

If the tourist occasionally creates problems for the State Department, that Department also at times creates problems for us little traveling bundles of good will. And when high officials have spoken to the world in phrases meant to tickle the ears of

"And Some of Those Countries Aren't American At All"

4/24/1953

"You Remember Us. We Helped In The 1952 Campaign"

5/9/1954

"I May Just Yank Out The Whole Thing"

7/8/1954

a Knowland or a Know-nothing, many Americans have wished
that the words were spoken privately, with less confusion to
everybody.

"I'd Have Said To Those Reds, 'Now, See Here! . . .'"

3/12/1954

It's tough enough to cope with currencies and decide what to get for Aunt Elvira without figuring out what an unofficial "representative of the United States" should say about some of the goings-on in Washington.

"Goodness—Is That The Way I Look?"

9/26/1954

This unofficial representative faced fewer questions than many of his friends only because of an appalling ignorance of languages. You can't get into long discussions about the home front when you're the kind of linguist who has to pad down four flights of stairs to hand a phone number to an operator, and then race back up with your little heart beating like a tom-tom, hoping that whoever answers the call will be able to understand either your English or your limited number of foreign phrases.

I wouldn't have liked to explain, in any language, the "unfortunate incidents" depicted in some of these cartoons, particularly at a time when the burning of a few books by State Department libraries made the free world feel that smoke got in its eyes. And I wouldn't know how to explain the actions of some of McCarthy's little playmates whom the State Department continues to employ in key positions. Even with a first-class translator there would be difficulty in describing how passport, visa and immigration sections of the Department demonstrated our opposition to Iron Curtain practices by trying to imitate them.

A domestic political hassle like l'affaire Corsi was read in foreign papers by people with a keen interest in our immigration policies.

In January 1955 Edward Corsi had come to Washington as Special Assistant to Secretary Dulles on immigration problems. He was filled with a high resolve to speed up the admission of refugees under a program which had become Operation Hope Deferred. At that time Dulles had referred to Corsi as "my dear friend" and had hailed him as "the best qualified man in the United States" for the job. He may have been just that. But after three months of coping with Security Pooh-Bah and Refugee Relief Director W. Scott McLeod, who did not seem to share his enthusiasm, Corsi was tossed out with the explanation that his appointment had been only a temporary one. Mr. Corsi, somewhat bewildered, said, "I never came down here asking for any job. Mr. Dulles, in a personal telegram, requested me to take on the work. I came down solely relying on the integrity and honesty of Mr. Dulles."

It's not at all improbable that some people abroad who also rely on the integrity and honesty of a U. S. Secretary of State might have gone through an agonizing reappraisal when they read that.

"Awful Lot Of Nationalism Abroad"

8/31/1953

Politics, our politicians often announce loftily, stops at the water's edge. That's what *they* say. But it often pauses at the brink only to brace itself for a leap across oceans. Sometimes it

"You Sure Everything's All Right, Foster?"

5/24/1954

even goes in for round-trip broad jumping. An interesting example of this was contained in a United Press dispatch from Rome in February 1954. This told of an article by former Italian Premier

"Well,
We Were Just Burning
A Few Books, And—"

6/26/1953

"It Seems To Be
Stopped Up Somewhere"

2/10/1954

1953
EMERGENCY
IMMIGRATION
ACT
TO ADMIT
209,000
REFUGEES

4
REFUGEES
IN
7 MONTHS

U.S.A.

147

"But My Friend Mr. Dulles Was Right Behind Me"

4/10/1955

Alcide de Gasperi which the UP said was interpreted as a bid
for more American aid. In this article the former Premier denied
that his party had been responsible for the rise of Communism

in Italy and said that Communism there "was born and prospered in the Roosevelt climate."

That seemed a pretty surprising reference for De Gasperi to make to the American President who had been so largely responsible for liberating Italy. It was one he could hardly have made had he felt it would be received with displeasure by the current powers in the United States; and it seemed to me to reflect more on the 1954 climate in Washington than on anything else.

In recent years we've often had a mixture of foreign policy and domestic politics which to many Europeans must have seemed like Chinese. This is not so surprising because a lot of it *has* been Chinese—Formosa Chinese.

The first big political move in foreign policy by the Eisenhower Administration was the "unleashing" of Chiang Kai-shek, early in 1953, when the President announced that the Seventh Fleet would no longer be used to "defend" Communist China. This implication that the previous Administration had been protecting Communist China may have been considered hot stuff by the politicians in Washington, but it was not warmly received by our allies, who are not members of the We Love Chiang Club, or the Hate Roosevelt And Truman Club either.

Our officials did a lot of traveling to Chiang, but Chiang did no traveling back to the mainland of China. He was in the spot of a man who has been hollering "Stop holding me. Lemme at him!" and who is suddenly embarrassed to find that he's free to get a pasting. The Administration, for its part, found itself in the uncomfortable position of a man who has been proclaiming that "My boy'll kill 'im!" and who now hears his boy saying, "Let's *you* and him fight." So Chiang was finally "leashed" again, to the relief of just about everybody—especially our western allies.

Another case where party politics nudged out better foreign relations was in the release of the Yalta papers over the protests of the British government. This was one of the most painfully contrived leaks on record, and for a while it looked as if Mr. Dulles was going to have to blast a hole in his office wall and chalk arrows on the sidewalk to let those papers out. They got

**"I Weep For You," The Walrus Said: "I Deeply Sympathize."
With Sobs And Tears He Sorted Out Those Of The Largest
Size, Holding His Pocket Handkerchief Before His
Streaming Eyes**

4/29/1955

out not only to us but to everybody else, complete with private
conversations not generally included in such papers; and it may

be many years before heads of governments speak to each other with the same kind of frank informality.

Incidentally, just as a passing thought before we leave the lower Crimea, it's always struck me as interesting that the people

"What's Our Firm, Unswerving Asia Policy This Week?"

4/28/1954

"Okay—The Wraps Are Off"

2/3/1953

who shed the hottest political tears over our losses in Korea were the same ones who most roundly condemned the 1945 Yalta agreements, which were made to save American lives in Japan.

Among other things that were released and unleashed was a barrage of snappy phrases that sounded as if some of the ad-conscious men in Washington thought the world was going to be won in a slogan-writing contest. But when politicians come into office as "crusaders" I guess they feel obliged to sound crusading even if they don't march anywhere except to the mimeograph machines to pick up the latest releases.

We were, first of all, not just going to continue *containing* Communism—which lacked the proper positive connotation—but were going to "liberate" peoples. Liberation is something that's hard to come by without fighting, and to our friends abroad who remembered this, the phrases did not have quite the appeal they had for domestic politicians or lexicon warriors.

We had "seized the initiative," which seemed to consist of holding on to a dragon's tail; and Vice President Nixon said we were not going to be "nibbled to death" in small wars, although he later thought we might have to send troops to Indochina. All this was so confusing that it required interpretation right at home.

There's no question at all that there are people abroad who, as President Eisenhower said, think Americans are "immature diplomatically, impulsive, too proud of their strength, ready to fight, and I have a suspicion that these ideas were not dispelled by things like Mr. Dulles' atomic threat of "instant and massive retaliation" in Asia.

The phrases were trumpeted forth as if we expected the Iron Curtain to fall like the walls of Jericho. Unfortunately it did not, but the Indochinese fortress of Dienbienphu did. In a way it was also the fall of Fort Huckster, at least as far as the conduct of foreign affairs by instant and massive sloganization was concerned. And if nobody had been liberated from Communism, at least we were partially liberated from political catch phrases.

We were also, in 1953 and 1954, going to make our intentions crystal clear to China, but this policy was jettisoned somewhere in the not so crystal-clear waters of the Formosa Straits when we deliberately adopted a keep-'em-guessing policy about Quemoy and Matsu. I don't know how it was in Peiping, but the guessing was terrific here and in Europe, where people and

See—I've Started
The Big Push Already"

2/6/1953

"It's Just
As I Almost Said—"

5/8/1955

154

"Anchors Aweigh"

1/13/1955

governments were scared silly that we might jump into war over those Chinese coastal islands, which were essential to nothing.

Mr. Dulles then declared that we were not a "paper tiger" and

"Could I See You Alone A Minute?"

2/1/1955

made appropriate warlike noises. It seemed to me he might have done well to identify much earlier a paper tiger on the home front. This was the China Lobby bloc, a somewhat tattered tiger which had long been prowling around Washington scaring states-

"Maybe I Shouldn't Have Pulled The Trigger"

3/20/1955

"First Things First"

3/18/1955

"Shall We Talk Sense Now?"

5/14/1954

men. It consisted of Senator Knowland in the paper head, senators like Bridges and Jenner moving the paper body, and Senator McCarthy, in his decline, furiously lashing the paper tail.

These men were prepared to give their all—or *our* all—for Chiang Kai-shek. To paper tigers of this stripe, negotiation was appeasement, and they glowered at proposals of East-West meetings—which took place anyhow, thanks to the persistent urgings of Churchill, Eden, and Senator George.

Happily, at this writing—which is being done with crossed fingers, making it a little difficult to type—we are apparently moving somewhat away from the Chiangs and the Bao Dais, who for a long time seemed to represent to Asians what we stood for in that part of the world. I recall an old Mutt and Jeff strip in which Mutt asked Jeff if he'd care to go along on a double date with a couple of girls. Jeff replied sadly, "Nah—I

"Come On—Let's Take The Short Cut"
12/6/1954

always get the one with the thick glasses." I don't know why we have so often let the Communists tie in with popular native movements for independence and social progress while we've as often been left with unpopular government heads who suffer from the worst kind of political astigmatism.

It's ironic that some of our government officials who are so sold on salesmanship and publicity shouldn't have done better than they have in winning friends and influencing people abroad. But, as early directors of our information programs discovered several years ago, the techniques for selling sudsy soap or even snowy-white political candidates are not the best ones for selling democracy and the U. S. of A.

"Hello—Ike?"

2/15/1955

"I Don't Know, Fella—I'm A Stranger Here Myself"

3/11/1955

President Eisenhower's atoms-for-peace proposal was an excellent idea, and one which, for a time at least, took the emphasis away from atomic destruction. Later, at the Geneva Conference

"Just Try It On For Size"
9/15/1954

of 1955, he seized the initiative from his own Secretary of State and Senate party leader to impress all hands with our earnest desire for peace. This desire has been so intense in our country that it might have been made obvious to the world much earlier had it not been obscured by official bluff and bluster, and big talk about our big bombs. And less than a week after the Summit Meeting the Japanese government was expressing unhappy surprise over an announcement from Washington that atomic cannon and rockets were being unloaded at Okinawa.

To our military and budget planners, baby A-bombs may be conventional weapons, but to most of the world these babies are little monsters that might usher in full-size atomic war. And the

"Come Come, Now—Let's See How Clever You Are"
3/26/1954

threat of that international nightmare has been associated mostly with one country—ours. This has not been due to our tourists, who seldom step down the gangplank onto foreign soil waving atomic bombs or shouting about them.

The words about these weapons have come from the U. S. and from U. S. officials; and why there should be so much yakking about them I don't know, because they don't need a big publicity build-up to impress either our friends or our enemies. They can speak for themselves and sometimes do it so loud they drown out almost everything else and scare the bejeebers out of our allies.

Of course, armament has been necessary. But a constant, unremitting emphasis on it hasn't been. There's a difference between

"We Interrupt This News
To Bring You
The Latest Chapter
Of 'John's Other
Amendment'—"

5/2/1955

"I'll Just Leave It Here
If You Want To Use It"

4/13/1955

164

Conference Seat

8/26/1953

"These Have Been Very Trying Days, Francois"

5/3/1955

keeping a revolver handy for emergency use and twirling one while talking to the neighbors. It makes them uncomfortable.

After all, nobody is endeared to the guy who seems fascinated by nothing more than his own muscles—or to the kind of statesmen who act as if every handshake was a preliminary to an Indian-wrestling match. If there's going to be any weight thrown among friends, it might better be tossed in the direction of some of the backward boys in our own bailiwick. World leadership begins at home.

When congressmen sink the knife into vital appropriations for U. S. or UN technical assistance programs; when they cripple student-exchange programs; or when high tariff groups bore loopholes into trade bills, it's not always enough to say, "Honest, fellows, we wish you wouldn't do that." The President and the Secretary of State can go to the mat with obstructionists, if they want to. And they can go to the people, via radio and TV, with issues as well as with success stories. They can let everybody know what's at stake in these programs and can let our friends abroad know how strongly our government feels about them. It's nice to get along with every member of Congress, but it's even nicer to get along with the rest of the world, which is bigger and more permanent.

We can also cut out the pandering to know-nothings who think that governments which don't cheer our every word must be Communistic, and we can eliminate the kind of politics which implies that statesmen of either party would "sell us out" or have been "taken in" by other governments. That kind of dangerous demagogy only increases fears about negotiating with anybody.

The greatest nation in the world is hardly an innocent abroad, and it needs to be said out loud that in the world today the danger of our being overly cunning or overly cautious is at least as great as the danger of our being too openhanded.

There may have been a day when the fate of peoples was settled by a few shrewd men sitting around a table, peering over maps, and taking pinches of snuff. But we're not dealing with pieces on a chessboard these days. We're dealing with millions of men and women who have their own ideas about the kind

166

"Shouldn't The Bodyguard Stay More In The Background?"

5/31/1955

of world they want to live in. They are not going to be won by words alone or by tourists, even on their best behavior. The United States itself has to be on its best behavior.

5/8/1953

There's no handy-dandy guidebook for Uncle Sam in Many
Lands or Etiquette in the Nuclear Age. But the ideals we pro-
claimed in 1776 still look awfully good, particularly to those

"Backward People"

1/2/1955

people in other parts of the world who are filled with the same
enthusiasm for independence, freedom and equality that inspired
us. Those ideals are still our greatest weapons, but they can't be

"We'll Import From Anywhere But Abroad"

4/19/1953

secret weapons. And our success in the world may depend most of all on how well we demonstrate our belief in our own professed principles.

"Squanderer!"

8/2/1954

Whatever progress is made in high-level conferences it might not be a bad idea to remember that there is a goal even beyond agreements between big-power leaders.

"We Saved Four Million Dollars On The U. N. Technical Assistance Program"

4/11/1955

The charter of the United Nations begins, "We, the peoples . . ." which are good words to paste in our hats. They can remind us that we're not only trying to reach heads of states, but *people.*

"Anybody Home Here?"

4/30/1954

Brief Encounter

5/26/1954

173

12/8/1953

This calls for more than craftiness or diplomatic finesse. It requires a real concern for the welfare of people, not as potential "native gun-bearers," and not merely as subjects of government or objects of propaganda, but as human beings. The Communist appearance of solicitude for the underprivileged can be beaten by one thing—the genuine article.

Whatever the diplomatic weather charts show the changing East-West climate to be, it seems certain that coexistence will at least be competitive. And even if Communism presented no threat at all, a great people concerned about world peace and peace of mind could hardly go wrong in working to improve the lot of their fellow men.

"You Were Always A Great Friend Of Mine, Joseph"

3/5/1953

8. OUTSIDE THAT CURTAIN

SINCE the Soviet government put some doors in the Iron Curtain there has been a rash of firsthand accounts describing conditions in Russia. But long before that we had analyses in the newspapers, and on radio and TV, of what was going on in the Kremlin and even inside the minds of the men in the Kremlin.

When Stalin died, the air waves were filled for days with inside dope and predictions about what this event meant. My view was that, if the reports from Moscow were accurate, Stalin was indeed dead and was no longer in charge. This threw no new light on events in Russia but added nothing to the general confusion either.

I didn't predict the rise, fall and survival of Georgi Malenkov, or the fact that in a little more than two years Molotov would be touring the U. S. wearing a ten-gallon cowboy hat. I couldn't say exactly what dictated the decision that the new Communist line should be the upturned curve of a smile—or why the Russians continued to display this pleasant smile when President Eisenhower proposed mutual aerial reconnaissance of military establishments, whereas Vishinsky had said in 1951 that he couldn't sleep for laughing at our proposals for international arms inspection.

All I know about what's really going on inside the Kremlin is that newspaper accounts report the government leaders are moving out of there with a view to converting it back to a museum. When that change is completed we will all know what's going on inside the Kremlin—which will be that Mama will want to look at more of the paintings, and Junior will scuff his feet and want to go home.

The following cartoons relating to the men in the Kremlin— or the men who *used* to be in the Kremlin—appeared during the

"—And It's Practically A Lifetime Appointment"

12/4/1952

period between Stalin and the Summit. They represent strictly outside dope, and were done without even getting close to a samovar.

Some of the principal characters have been inclined to be fictional, and all of them are subject to change without notice.

**"Why, Yes—
I Knew Lavrenti Beria"**

7/14/1953

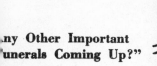

**ny Other Important
'unerals Coming Up?"**

'10/1953

179

"Sickle"

7/12/1953

". . . The Defendants, Beria, Dekanozov, Meshik . . ."

12/20/1953

6/19/1953

"Who's Cooking, Comrade?"

7/6/1953

"Never Mind Wrapping Them—We'll Use Them Here"

7/20/1953

3/29/1954

"You Mean You Won't Swear Me In As A Deputy?"

4/6/1954

"As A Final Offer, I'll Give You Time To Reconsider"

11/23/1954

"Ever Listen To The Radio, Comrade?"

2/9/1955, following Malenkov's resignation from the number-one position

"Well, Circumstances Alter Cases"

5/22/1955

**"Hey—
A Plain Handshake
Is Enough"**

5/29/1955

"Hey—Watch That Shoving, Will You?"

6/24/1955

"Molotov To Kremlin—Am I Still Defrosting?"

6/30/1955

"It's Really More Of A 2-Power Conference, Ain't It?"

7/11/1955

9. THE CLOUD AND THE SUMMIT

ON July 9, 1955, nine days before the Big Four conference opened at Geneva, Bertrand Russell issued a statement signed by the late Albert Einstein and seven other noted scientists, speaking as "members of the species man, whose continued existence is in doubt." It said, in part:

> The world is full of conflicts; and overshadowing all minor conflicts, the titanic struggle between Communism and anti-Communism.
>
> We have to learn to think in a new way. We have to learn to ask ourselves, not what steps can be taken to give military victory to whatever group we prefer, for there no longer are such steps, the question we have to ask ourselves is: What steps can be taken to prevent a military contest of which the issue must be disastrous to all parties?
>
> The general public, and even many men in position of authority, have not realized what would be involved in a war with nuclear bombs. . . .
>
> No doubt in an H-bomb war great cities would be obliterated. But this is one of the minor disasters that would have to be faced.
>
> If everybody in London, New York and Moscow were exterminated the world might, in the course of a few centuries, recover from the blow.
>
> But we now know, especially since the Bikini test, that nuclear bombs can gradually spread destruction over a much wider area than had been supposed.
>
> It is stated on very good authority that a bomb can

now be manufactured which will be 2500 times as powerful as the bomb which destroyed Hiroshima.

Such a bomb, if exploded near the ground or under water, sends radioactive particles into the upper air. They sink gradually and reach the surface of the earth in the form of a deadly dust or rain. It was this dust which infected the Japanese fishermen and their catch of fish.

No one knows how widely such lethal radioactive particles might be diffused, but the best authorities are unanimous in saying that a war with H-bombs might quite possibly put an end to the human race. . . .

Here, then, is the problem which we present to you, stark and dreadful, and inescapable:

Shall we put an end to the human race, or shall mankind renounce war? . . .

The abolition of war will demand distasteful limitation of national sovereignty. But what perhaps impedes understanding of the situation more than anything else is that the term "mankind" feels vague and abstract. . . .

People scarcely realize in imagination that the danger is to themselves and their children and their grandchildren, and not only to a dimly apprehended humanity. . . .

Most of us are not neutral in feeling, but, as human beings, we have to remember that, if the issues between East and West are to be decided in any manner that can give any possible satisfaction to anybody, whether Communist or anti-Communist, whether Asian or European or American, whether white or black, then these issues must not be decided by war. . . .

H-BOMB

HERBLOCK
©1953 THE WASHINGTON POST Co.

8/11/1953

193

"Think Maybe We'd Better Say Something About It?"

8/10/1953

"1945—46—47—48—49—50—51—52—53—54—"

1/1/1954

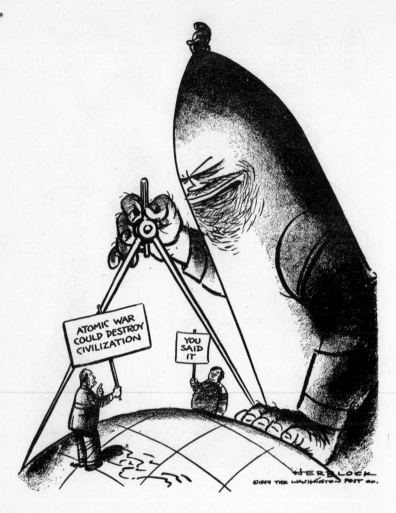

Area Of Agreement

4/29/1954

"And What's New With You?"

4/25/1954

"It Looks Darling"

9/3/1954

Shape Of Things To Go

2/20/1955

A Cloud No Bigger Than A Man's Future

3/9/1955

"Hey—Maybe A Parking Place"

5/19/1955

"Yes, We'll Be There, Rain And Shine"

7/4/1955

"Pretty Good—How Have Things Been Going With You?"

7/17/1955

**"This Sure Beats
Cleaning Up
After A War"**

7/25/1955

"Not Yet, But Save It"

8/8/1955

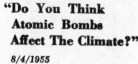

"Do You Think Atomic Bombs Affect The Climate?"

8/4/1955

7/19/1955

The Other Door

8/11/1955

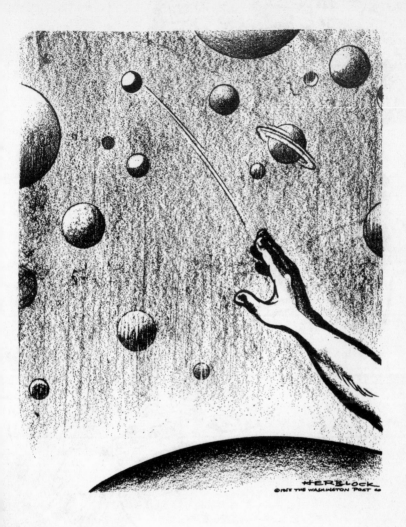

Big League Ball

7/31/1955, on the announcement that man-made satellites were to be constructed

"We're Always Willing To Bargain"

9/19/1955

9/23/1955

"I Don't Want To Complain, But You Never Take Me Anywhere"

11/1/1955

"And Next, Mates, We Head For Land"

4/15/1953

10. BUSINESS LETTER

BOARD OF DIRECTORS,
U. S. POLICY MANUFACTURING CO.,
WASHINGTON, D. C.

GENTLEMEN:

For as long as I can remember I've been hearing that the running of the U. S. A. was a business, and one in which we should employ businessmen, using business methods.

I never was able to find *U. S. A. com.*, or *America, Inc.* listed on the exchange, even when the Coolidge Administration told us not to sell America short; and that, plus the fact that I didn't have any money on hand, may have saved me a few dollars when things fell off in 1929. But I know that everything isn't listed on the boards, and a lot of transactions take place more or less quietly these days anyhow.

A great deal of what I've heard about the Budget and Economy and the U. S. Company, as I guess you'd call it, has come from solid, hardheaded, practical, and thoroughly respectable people too—not idle dreamers or visionaries. "It's the biggest Business in the world," they've always said, "and we're all shareholders in it."

I'm just a very small shareholder in that business, but I've been with the Firm for over 45 years now, and I hope you won't think it presumptuous of me to write you fellows on the Board of Directors, because there are a few things I'd like to bring up.

You gentlemen have often explained that our U. S. Company had to be run by men who had met payrolls in other companies, which certainly sounds logical if we're a big Business. I understand that our present Chairman of the Board didn't have much experience at payroll meeting before he got his present position, but you fellows seem to like him pretty well; and as practical, realistic men you must certainly know what you're doing. I think it's fine that you're not hidebound or inflexible in your ideas, and that's why I'm taking the liberty of making some suggestions farther on.

I'm not much of a businessman, but there are some things that have been bothering me about the Company, and I might as well come right out and tell you. I began to wonder in 1953, when our Company signed away all that off-shore property, which I understand was worth billions of dollars and which the Supreme Court had ruled belonged to us. This didn't seem to me to be a businesslike thing to do. I don't know of any other company that would hand over property like that, and I don't see how we can get ahead that way.

You might say that this was some old underwater stuff we never used much and that it was just cluttering up the books. Still, it was evidently valuable to other firms, and I'd think a big company like ours might have made something out of it. I remember at the time Lister Hill said we could have got enough money out of that property to improve all our school plants. But we let it go. I don't think we were being very economical there.

It's the same way with some of our other properties, in parks, forests and public lands. If our directors are going to keep giving things away, we're going to be losing ground all the time— and a lot of it valuable ground that can't be replaced. At the rate we're going, we're liable to end up with nothing but a chimney and a few advertising leaflets.

I don't understand how businessmen can operate that way. Maybe some of them who spent a lot of time with other companies have had a hard time getting used to the idea that they're working for us now. This must be particularly difficult for some of the men who work for us and for other businesses at the same time.

Many of our officials seem remarkably unenthusiastic about some of our most successful items. I mean a thing like that public power we've been producing.

"What'll It Be Today,
Fellows?"

213

"Don't Peek—It's Sort Of A Surprise"

5/4/1955

I can't remember anything we've put out that was so success-ful. No other company could possibly have done what we did there or could have made it work nearly so well. We opened up

U.S. FOREST LANDS

"GRAZING BILL"

PRIVATE INTEREST GRABS

HERBLOCK
©1954 THE WASHINGTON POST CO.

"Kind Sir, I Am A Poor Little Shepherd Maid"

5/10/1954

whole new territories and got that power to people who never had it before—and at reasonable rates. The new customers were amazed by what it could do. It wouldn't be putting it too strongly

215

"Take A Letter"

7/22/1955

to say that they were electrified. Down around Tennessee that power even helped us develop the atom bombs, which are among our most talked-of products. Next thing you know I suppose

"We Must Stop This Federal Interference"

7/30/1954

"What's The Matter? I Didn't Get A Mink Coat"

7/29/1955

217

somebody'll want to turn *those* over to other business concerns too.

Well, what's been happening with that power manufacturing of ours? We haven't been doing anything much about it since 1952, despite the big demand and the fact that other companies can't meet that demand the way we can, although they turn a handsome profit themselves. Some of our directors want us to discontinue that line altogether or let other companies handle the distribution and make all the money on our product. It just doesn't figure.

We're supposed to have top-notch businessmen running things for us now. But a member of our Interior Department admitted that this Department had made changes in electric-power regulations which were practically copied from a memorandum mailed out by a private utilities company. We don't need high-class businessmen for that. A messenger boy could do as well. This doesn't seem to me to represent that *initiative* we've always heard about.

Another thing I don't understand is those "partnerships" we've been getting into. There's been a lot of talk about partnership lately, and I guess I'm not so familiar with the term as you businessmen. I always thought that partnership meant a fifty-fifty divvying-up kind of thing. But in some of those power partnerships, we seem to be putting up half the money while some other company gets all the profits. I'm surprised that the businessmen running our U. S. Company would get us into partnerships like that, especially when we're so much in debt.

Our directors don't seem to have much get-up or pride in our company. If the other fellows at the country club needle them and say, "Oh, you eager beavers and your dams," you'd think our men would get right into the spirit of the thing and say, "Undersell us, boy. We love competition!" They could smile like they do in the newspaper pictures, give the other fellows an elbow in the ribs, and say, "You boys don't seem to be doing so bad yourselves."

But no. They get apologetic and try to figure out more ways to let the other companies use our property, and don't seem to think about us "little shareholders" at all. Somebody is always

"But First A Few Words From Our Sponsors"

7/27/1955

saying that we're saps when we give food to hungry people somewhere, but I don't see what's so smart about giving away our valuables to millionaires.

"This Is The Only Guy Who's Entitled To Bargain Rates"

7/3/1955

There's still a terrific unsatisfied demand for power, particularly in the Northwest and in some of the rural areas where we seem to be trying to cut down. I think we ought to be doing something to keep that line moving.

Creeping Localism

4/1/1954

I've been meaning to write for a long time, and while I'm at it I might as well tell you something else I don't like—that's all the secrecy in our Company. I don't mean just about the atom products, although I've felt we ought to know more about those

"First Thing To Do Is Take Down Those Damn Plaques"

5/30/1954

too, just in case the competition should ever decide to get into our territory. For a company with as many shareholders as there are in ours, I think there ought to be fuller reports on a lot of things.

I don't think an outfit like ours ought to go in for under-the-counter stuff. People like Mr. Dixon and Mr. Yates and their friends may be nice guys, and I'm not against business. But I don't like monkey business. I think our Executive Office should put out less publicity stuff and more information. I think we're entitled to find out who—including us—is getting the business.

One thing I know is that the business methods we've been using lately don't seem to be working very well; and a former Chairman of the Board, Mr. Hoover, seems to feel we should have a big going-out-of-business sale. If we're not any good at business, we ought to get into something else. That's why I've got up a plan that I want to suggest.

What I think we need is a whole new approach to things. We've still got all those buildings in Washington and elsewhere, and there's no use wasting them or waiting for them to be given away. All of them could be used under the system I have in mind, which would be called not a business but a "government." This comes from the Latin word *gubernare*, meaning "to govern"; but I don't want anyone to get scared and think there's anything un-American about my proposal.

When I say government, a lot of you are going to ask "What on earth is that? What crazy idea has this fellow thought up?" I won't go into all the details of my plan, which is pretty long and involved. But it would keep the present departments of the business just about as they are now. Our Capitol Hill branch, which has been handling so much of our investigative research in recent years, could continue with that on a smaller scale but would work more to represent the shareholders—or "citizens," as I'd call them. Incidentally, I didn't think that idea of doing some research into the stock market was so terrible, although some of the Company officials seemed rather alarmed about it. There's no harm in knowing a little about shareholding in other companies too. Well, to get on . . .

The Executive branch of the Firm would remain pretty much as it is, except that there might be some changes on the business-man's luncheon plate and in some of the men around the plates.

Hell's Canyon

8/10/1955

As a brief prospectus I've written out a few objectives here
to show what we'd be trying to get at under this system.

First of all, in a giant organization like ours, scattered all over

"How Long Do You Think It'll Stay Radioactive?"

11/7/1954

the landscape, we might try to form what I'd call "a more perfect Union." Now, don't go flying off the handle—this has nothing to do with labor organizing. I'm thinking about those 48 areas we've

"The Top Top One?
That's The Dixon-Yates
Contract"

10/8/1954

"Hurry, Friend—
There's Not
A Moment To Lose"

11/12/1954

"I've Stopped—Now Let's Forget The Whole Thing"
7/16/1955

got marked out on the chart, which we might even want to boost to 50 one of these days, although our present Chairman of the Board hasn't been much for expansion recently. I know

"It Looks Wonderful—And It'll Wear Like Iron"

5/18/1955

that most of our present directors like to parcel things out to these 48 areas and to other businesses in those areas, but that hasn't worked well in a lot of cases; and I think we might as well face the fact that we're a big outfit now and we're all in it together.

We'd also want to "Establish Justice" and "insure domestic Tranquility." Already I can hear some people say that this is purely visionary, that you can't have Security under a system of that kind. But I think we can, and have pretty well covered this in my next aim, which is to provide for the common defense. Incidentally, if it'll relieve any of your fears about my plan, I'd have plenty of defense materials—in some departments maybe even more than we've been getting.

What we'd really be trying to do would be to "promote the general Welfare," and, to end on a forward-looking note, to "secure the Blessings of Liberty to ourselves and our Posterity."

That Welfare part may run into the greatest opposition of all. I know you're thinking this sounds like madness. "Business is business," you're going to tell me. "What's all this nonsense about Welfare?" But, remember, you're still thinking in the old terms and haven't got used to this new idea of "government" yet. However, I'd like to point out that some of the other businesses you most admire have hospitalization and things of that sort. Even in our own U. S. Company our officials in Washington enjoy such benefits and are always running over to Bethesda Naval Hospital for checkups and free medical care. I'd just extend some of the same kind of benefits to take in more shareholders—or people—throughout the present firm.

This doesn't mean that we need to plunge into the kind of thing that foreign radicals like Churchill and Eden have been willing to stand for. But there's no use kidding around either. I won't make any bones about the fact that in this "government" I'd have a regular Welfare Department which would promote things like Health, Education and Welfare, instead of making sure we didn't get too much of them. To that extent my plan would involve a complete reversal of what we've been doing.

Suppose, for example, that somebody should come up with a new kind of vaccine that everybody was interested in. This Welfare Department would plan ahead to see that it was prop-

**"Okay—
Cut Out The Laughing
And Let's Read This"**

1/18/1955

**"It Never Existed—
And I Killed It"**

7/20/1954

"He's Perfectly Healthy—Just Terribly Sensitive"

3/15/1955

erly developed and tested and made available to people who needed it. Of course, this wouldn't be a completely new idea, because our U. S. Company previously did that with yellow-fever

"Very Interesting—You Must Come Again Some Time"

5/12/1955

vaccine—and nearly 150 years ago, took a hand in the distribution of smallpox vaccine.

This Welfare Department could also take the same kind of interest in education. I don't mean the way the businessmen in

HERBLOCK
©1954 THE WASHINGTON POST CO.

"Try This On For Size And See Me Again Next Year"

8/1/1954

our Firm have done it, by making up high-sounding financial plans for the 48 local outfits to borrow money which they can't afford to borrow.

Under my plan we'd figure that the kids were all part of our

233

Conclusion

5/20/1955

growing outfit—future personnel, you might say—and we'd figure it was worth spending something to train them. Or, in straight business terms, you might regard them as a resource that's worth

**"Rest Assured That If We Find One Polio Germ Crossing
A State Line—"**

5/13/1955

developing. You fellows know how businesses write off things
for depreciation and how they get to expand their plants and
all. Well, the school plants have depreciated to a point where

"Glad To Help—Here's Some Swimming Lessons"

2/10/1955

they can't turn out the product as well as they ought to, and a lot of them are unsafe besides.

A "government" would be interested in things like that and

I think quite a few of our Capitol Hill men would fit right in with the idea I'm trying to explain here.

As a matter of fact, the new system wouldn't really involve a tremendous change-over, because our Firm is already in the welfare field. But our directors seem to do a lot of worrying about it, and act as if it were immoral or something. Some of them keep wanting us to cut out everything we've been doing in that line.

The whole trouble, as I see it, is that our directors haven't been able to make up their minds about this Business business—about what business we're in, or why we're in it. When we make money on something, or break even, they feel that we should stop and let some other business do it. And when we operate something that doesn't pay its way, they complain that it's *not* making money.

Now, take that postal business we run. They've cut down on the service, which has been terrible lately; and they keep saying that the parcel-post department, for example, isn't *paying*.

Under my plan they could stop chewing their pencils, shaking their heads and figuring how to whittle down the service some more. They could figure that as a "government" we were trying to make it easy for our people to communicate with one another. We wouldn't *have* to show a profit on everything. We could say it's for the people, and any deficit would be charged up to the people in the annual assessments.

I haven't quite got it into a phrase or slogan yet, but what I have in mind is that this "government" idea would be something for all the people. Of course, it would also be government *of* them and *by* them at the same time. I'll have to polish that up a little more to make it sound better.

Well, this whole idea of "governing" would depend a lot on the personnel. We'd need to have people who were willing to "govern"—or control, direct and regulate, as Webster says. You remember how the men in our Federal Power Commission office said they couldn't regulate prices for natural gas sold to interstate pipelines, and how the Supreme Court had to tell them

"Here I Am, Mister"

7/19/1954

they should *so*. Our Executive Department seems to have appointed a lot of commissioners like that lately, and the results haven't been so good for us little shareholders in the U. S. Company.

Latest Report From Behind The Iron Collar

4/26/1955

As a "government" we'd figure that our business was what you might call the "people's business." We'd be sort of a public-service institution.

We'd also figure that the lands and waters and forests we own

"Now You Take Good Care Of This Nice Fish"

6/17/1953

belong to all of us, and that it's the business of government officials to remember that.

This "government" would look after the interests of all share-

"Let's See, Now—Where Can We Raise More Taxes?"
9/7/1953

holders—or people—whether they were in business for themselves or not. We could keep on with the projects that people need and like, and we wouldn't have to worry when some of those

"Boy, We Could Develop That Into Some Fine Stumps"

3/15/1953

things don't make a profit, because we wouldn't really be operating for profit. We're not making a profit anyhow. And we wouldn't need to worry about the things that *did* make money because we could use that money to cut down our debts. I think that would solve a lot of problems that seem to have been bothering you fellows in the Company.

You might think this whole idea wouldn't be economical, but when you figure what we're giving away and what we've lost on loopholes in the Company assessments and everything, I'll bet we'd actually come out ahead.

Well, this has been a pretty long letter, and I know you fellows have a great many business appointments and a lot of work to do. But I hope you'll give some consideration to this little idea that I'm tossing into the "suggestion box," as you might say.

I just want you to know that one of the small shareholders is thinking about you and I hope you'll do some thinking about us too.

> Sincerely,
> H. BLOCK
> Shareholder (common)

The Bookworms

12/1/1952

11. WHAT DO YOU KNOW?

IN THE gangster movies somebody is always getting slugged or plugged with the simple explanation, delivered in a gravel voice: "We're getting rid of you. *You know too much.*" This line has the virtue of being frank and direct. The victim may get beaten about the head, but he is spared any beating about the bush. He is not accused of subversion, ostensibly conked in a search for Communism, or flattened for his own good. He just knows too much.

Many people lately have been expressing concern about the depiction of such violent scenes, and some of them are so devoted to our welfare that they would gouge our eyes out or kick our ears off to protect us from seeing or hearing anything they think might hurt us.

I'm not rising to defend a steady entertainment diet of lead-in-the-head or a thousand fascinating methods of mayhem for the kiddies; but I find these fictions less offensive than the trussing and torturing of Miss Liberty, or the figurative bumping off of people who know too much of Constitutional rights, science or things in general.

Nothing has appeared on entertainment screens half so obscene as the blacklisting practices and censorship devices that have kept people and pictures *off* those screens. No play or movie has been so noxious as some of the political performances which have committed cold, calculated assaults on the intellect. And a lot of the theatrical gangster types have been little gentlemen compared to some Congressional investigators who would plug an honest reputation as casually as they'd pull out a pencil.

Ideas are regarded as dangerous and learning has been shoved around by zealous persons who would solve all problems by tying on a gag or belting somebody on the noggin—and who seem to feel that any situation can be met with good old know-not. They

HERBLOCK
©1954 THE WASHINGTON POST CO.

"Fair Is Fair"
3/10/1954

constitute what might be called the yegghead school of thought,
if "school" and "thought" were not so inappropriate in connection with them.

These people are going to save us from Communism, from immorality and from the incalculable dangers of seeing, hearing and knowing too much. But most of all they are going to save us from ourselves. They feel they have a right and a duty to do this because they are so much smarter, so much better, and so much more loyal and patriotic than all the rest of us. These selfless souls are scattered around in local action groups, in state and city governments, and in Washington.

The Post Office Department may not be so good at delivering the mail these days, but it has worked to deliver us from temptation and evil, a chore that we used to ask Somebody Else to handle. Several years back, under a different Administration, this department was going to save us from the pictures of pretty girls in *Esquire*. But the Supreme Court ruled against that high-minded and higher-handed effort, with the result that today we are all presumably in danger of becoming sex-mad fiends while leafing through the magazines in the dentist's waiting room.

In 1955 this same department acted to save us from being demoralized by Aristophanes' comedy *Lysistrata*, a play which the world has somehow managed to survive, despite repeated performances since 411 B.C. The ban on *Lysistrata* was lifted when somebody whispered into the cauliflower ears of the authorities that it was a classic.

Official and unofficial censorship boards have spared no effort to save us from seeing movies that they regard as fit only for their own eyes. However, those devilish fellows on the U. S. Supreme Court, debauched by dipping into racy books on Constitutional law, have more than once stepped in to interfere with the censors' noble aims. It is only recently that newsreels have become exempt from censorship in all 48 states. Whither are we drifting? If this keeps up, people may have to decide for themselves what to see. It's almost enough to make the senses reel or make the reels sensible.

But the protection of our morals runs second to the protection of the American people from subversive thoughts. What would become of our freedom if people were allowed to read and dis-

"But It's Such An Old Routine"

8/14/1955

cuss all kinds of ideas? If we insist on exercising our liberties, how can those liberties be preserved—or, more accurately, pickled? The vigilantes are determined to leave no stone unturned or unthrown to protect us.

"For Heaven's Sake, Use More Restraint Than I Did"

11/24/1954

"Are You Now Or Have You Ever Been A Member Of An Un-American School?"

8/16/1954

3-D

1/20/1954

The postal authorities have not been idle in this work either.
Again in 1955 they acted to keep the American people from
going Communist as a result of reading *Pravda* and *Izvestia*, the

official Russian newspapers—which are, incidentally, printed in Russian.

These publications, which the Post Office withheld from all but an arbitrarily selected few, would not be likely to compete with our dailies for circulation even if a free bicycle were given with each copy. Former Ambassador George F. Kennan pointed out that such papers give us important clues as to what's going on behind the Iron Curtain, that a study of them would be more likely than anything else to *unsell* a reader on Communism, and—most important—that suppression of this kind is inconsistent with American freedom. But these are small matters to men determined that the mail must not go through.

Shortly after this Post Office Department action was announced, two United States senators moved to save us all from destroying ourselves when they proposed that *The Daily Worker* be banned. For all we know, this miserable paper may already be subverting the FBI men, who probably make up most of its ragged subscription list.

Those senators possibly felt that the real danger lies in people being able to read at all. Even those of us who read only English might be corrupted. And when people have a choice of ideas or arguments, how do you know they won't make the wrong choice? The yeggheads would solve this problem by making sure that there is no choice. That's the way it's done in—oh, yes—Russia.

Even apart from questions of constitutionality, such policies are an insult to the American people; and those who advocate them can't really believe much in the democracy they profess to be protecting. But the champions of Freedom to Suppress are sure they know what's best for us.

The executive branch of government, and particularly the Defense Department, has worked at withholding vital public information to a point where newspapers have complained of a "news brownout" or "gray censorship." The Defense Department has its own ideas of information, and in the spring of 1955 the public got a peek at an interesting little document which had originally been prepared by the First Army for some of its per-

Latest Master Stroke On The Security Front

3/10/1955

sonnel, and later was published as an article in the *Air Intelligence Training Bulletin* before public complaints compelled the Defense Department to end its distribution.

Titled "How to Spot a Communist," this article listed several words which it gave as helpful "clues" in Communist-spotting. Among them were *chauvinism, hootenanny, book-burning, colonialism, witch-hunting, reactionary, exploitation, hooliganism, imperialism* and *progressive.* Subjects which provided "danger signals" included *McCarthyism, violation of civil rights, racial or religious discrimination, immigration laws; any legislation concerning labor unions, the military budget* and *peace.*

The authors and distributors of that little gem might have done well to keep an eye on the entire U. S. ·Senate and House of Representatives, which in the summer of 1955 passed, without a dissenting vote, a resolution affirming that the United States should maintain its traditional policy against colonialism. Since the word "McCarthyism" evidently originated in one of my cartoons, I must certainly be suspect—along with everybody from President Eisenhower on down who has referred to "peace," "the military budget," "immigration laws" and most of the other words on the list. Congressmen, the entire AFL–CIO membership and all the supporters of the Taft-Hartley Act had better think twice before engaging in any further discussions of l-b-r l-g-sl-t-on. And if a woman driver refers to anything under the hood as a "hootenanny," follow that car!

Economy-minded executives could have saved the government the cost of printing and distributing that paper simply by whispering instructions to keep a sharp lookout for anyone who could pronounce words of three or more syllables.

Education itself seems to be the danger which the Knownothings are really trying to eliminate, and some have been more direct in going to the heart of the matter—or maybe I should say the head.

Private vigilante groups have long been busy attacking every form of progressive education, and undoubtedly assume that anything labeled progressive *and* educational must put us in double jeopardy. If a little learning is a dangerous thing, more learning must be more dangerous. A committee headed by Senator Jenner decided that the Upper House of Congress was the proper body

"You Know The Old Saying—No News Is Good News"

6/23/1955

to investigate higher education and went after the colleges and universities. Colleges are veritable hotbeds of learning. These are the places where ideas are propagated. And by whom? Teachers! Professors! Intellectuals!

"Sorry—He's Tied Up Right Now"

7/5/1955

All Quiet Along The Potomac

1/4/1955

"I'll Do All The Foolish Talking Around Here"

4/8/1955

The yeggheads do not, of course, say they wish to *attack* education. They only *investigate* it and put on a little pressure here and there to see that the schools and colleges get the idea.

"Sometimes I Wonder
What's In Those
Darn Things"

5/3/1953

"You're Not Here
To Think, Mister"

11/17/1954

257

They have what might be called a one-way interest in education, which can be symbolized by an EXIT sign. They are interested in throwing out teachers, students and books, but seldom show much concern about getting people *into* schools or providing sufficient school facilities for the students. They are hot after "reds" in the schools but unconcerned about the schools being in the red.

Congressman B. Carroll Reece carried the same type of endeavor into another field when he conducted, in 1954, an "investigation" aimed at the great private foundations engaged in education and research. He saw in the work of the Rockefeller Foundation and similar organizations a dastardly revolutionary threat to the Republic. Mr. Reece and a number of others seem to think that practically every group enterprise is socialistic, possibly including car pools. To them, free enterprise and rugged individualism are all right in the cash register, but not in the head. And as far as freedom of inquiry is concerned, they apparently feel that congressmen will ask all the questions around here.

But even Mr. Reece was outdone by Senator Eastland of Mississippi, who in 1955 became so unhappy about the U. S. Supreme Court's rulings against segregation in the schools that he asked for an investigation of Communist influence upon authorities relied on by the Court.

For the cave men among congressmen, charges of Communism are only convenient clubs to be used in beating out brains. Yeggheadism isn't just anti-liberal; it's anti-literate, and with good reason. To demagogues, education is really dangerous. It cuts down their votes and their support.

To the yeggheads we are all either dopey or dangerous; we should be treated like morons or should be ashamed of ourselves for *not* being morons. This is why they must keep a constant watch on us. They have been working for some time to make "intellectual" a dirty word, and would probably be scrawling it on fences if they knew how to spell it.

Many politicians seem to feel that a little genuflection to anti-intellectualism adds a nice folksy touch and does no harm at the ballot box. I think such gestures are no great political asset, and do harm to the country.

"You Got All Their Names?"

6/8/1953

During the 1954 campaign, President Eisenhower told a little joke about intellectualism: he'd heard that an intellectual is a "man who takes more words than necessary to tell more than

"I Can't Stand It, I Tell You. It's Driving Me Batty"

3/11/1953

he knows." For a man who frowned on humor in the previous campaign and who is not much given to joke-telling, I think he might have spared himself this one. At a time when education

"That's The Trouble With This Country—Foundations"

12/21/1954

and the centers of learning have been under attack, a President of the United States—particularly one who had served a brief term as President of Columbia University on the way—might even

"I Guess They're Trying To Sell Us On Socialism"

6/7/1954

have done something to turn back the tide of know-nothingism by speaking up *for* intellectualism.

There's no reason to think that this would be politically hazardous, despite the myth, spread after the 1952 campaign, that any intellectual appeal was a political handicap. Americans are not really the knuckleheads that some of the political sharpies seem to think. In the past 50 years the two men who served longest in the White House were Woodrow Wilson, historian and Princeton University professor, and Franklin D. Roosevelt, who had enough regard for intellectualism to display his trust in brains publicly in a "brain trust." Wilson and Roosevelt did not even conceal the fact that they were on speaking terms with the classics.

This is as good a place as any to toss in a classic quote. Plato said that "what is honored in a country is cultivated there." Whatever we've been honoring lately, it doesn't seem to be education. Even science and engineering have been suffering, and they are important to the military needs for which we have, if not honor, at least a healthy respect. Atomic Energy Commissioner Willard Frank Libby warned, in May 1955, that "the shortage of adequately trained scientists and engineers is a matter of serious concern to the nation." He added that the cause of this situation went back to the high-school level.

It's no coincidence that public men who do not seem to think too highly of higher learning fail us also at the lower educational level. If learning is dangerous or unimportant, there's no use subjecting the kids to too much of it. And look at the money you save.

But there are books more important than those labeled BUDGET; and the road to learning must be kept in as good repair as motor highways.

In this decade we've been in an educational crisis which is as serious in its way as the economic crisis of the thirties. There is a hunger today, not for food but for learning. The good old ways of the good old days which flopped so miserably in the economic depression also failed to relieve the educational depression.

Agnes E. Meyer, one of the country's foremost authorities on schools, as well as one of its greatest champions of education, has estimated that a billion dollars a year of Federal aid, for the next five years, is needed for our schools to keep pace with the rising population and make up for twenty years of neglect.

**"We Can't Subpoena
Him. I Think He's
On Our Staff"**

11/24/1953

**"Thanks For
The Compliment"**

8/19/1954

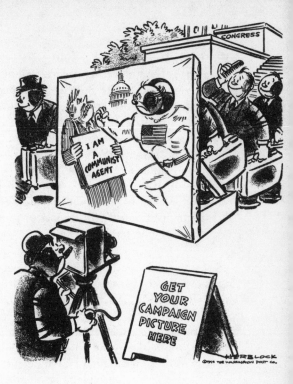

**"Step Lively, Gents—
Next—Okay, Next—"**

8/18/1954

**"What's This
About Your Letting
The Common People
Come In Here
And Read Books?"**

6/6/1954

265

Of a total eleven billions required for school construction alone, she said that the states can meet only about 55 per cent of the costs.

Testifying before the Senate Subcommittee on Education in 1954, Mrs. Meyer declared:

> The Duke of Wellington said after the Battle of Waterloo that this victory, which saved the freedom of Europe from Napoleon's domination, was won on the playing fields of Eton. It is my carefully considered opinion that the freedom of our country and therefore of the non-Communist world will be lost or preserved in the classrooms of our public schools.

A whopping federal program for school construction and teaching is a necessity for the children, and it might have good effects on adults as well. The focusing of national attention on schools could remind us of the importance of learning and put new life into dispirited intellectuals—a term which has lately come to be applied to almost anyone with a reasonable respect for learning.

Many of those who should have been defending intellectualism have been either in retreat or in a state of shock. Too many of them have not only hung their heads but tried to hide them. College administrators have "welcomed" investigations of education by yeggheads who investigate with hatchets. Intelligent men and women have not cried out enough about the rewriting of history. Many have been apologetic about their ideas and their ideals—including the worthy and even noble hope of twenty years ago that democratic government might be preserved in Spain. And they have felt obliged to separate themselves from proper and legitimate organizations.

School authorities have too often avoided controversy, and they have remained silent when potential corporate employers publicly warned students to avoid controversial discussions. University heads have even canceled engagements of distinguished speakers because someone growled the frightening mumbo-jumbo words "controversial figure." They have endured censorship, boycotts and attacks without striking back. They have been meek

"Run Along And Shoot Pool Or Something"

5/17/1954

before the yeggheads and thanked them when the bruises and concussions were relatively minor.

"Tread upon a worm and it will turn." Bookworms can do as

"Shoo!"

4/21/1955

much; and they'd better, before they feel obliged to receive their magazines in "plain wrappers," keep their books in the basement, conceal poetry volumes inside copies of the Racing Form, and

"Yeah, Uh Huh, Sounds Fine"

1/18/1955

practice moving their lips when they read, to avoid seeming too intelligent.

There has been too much worry about being "over the heads"

"Sometimes We Almost Feel Like Giving The Kids A Break"

7/4/1954

of Americans. I'm tired of hearing people "talk down." I'd like to hear more talking up and talking back. I want to see literate people lean into the face of yegghead tyranny and say, "We're

"How Can You Learn Lessons In Here? Why, There's Hardly Room For *You*, And No Room At All For Any Lesson Books!"—*Alice in Wonderland*

2/24/1955

getting rid of you. *You don't know enough!"*

There is an American answer for the censors, for the bully boys who want to put the strong-arm on education and the arts,

"Stand Fast, Men—They're Armed With Marshmallows"
8/11/1954

for the know-nothings and the politicians who make their pitch to them. It does not involve polysyllabic words, or, in fact, any words at all. It is a long, loud Bronx cheer. That, to use one of

Richest Country In The World

9/8/1953

their own phrases, is something they can understand.

It's time to throw the book at them—making sure, of course, that it's not over their heads.

School Bell

5/19/1954

"Yeah, He Was Always A Guy That Liked Freedom"

1/16/1953, on President Truman's departure from office.

"On The Other Hand, He Doesn't Look Very Sleepy"

4/3/1955, on the news of Churchill's imminent retirement

"He Gets Off A Nice Clear Decision, Doesn't He?"

4/17/1955

"Of Course I Know—It's Mrs. Roosevelt"

10/11/1954, in celebration of Mrs. Roosevelt's 70th birthday